"As I read through this book, I s[...] [...]self, 'Why has nobody done this before?' The book is full of how to learn and what
to learn, and all very neatly classified and presented. Jeff very
evidently knows what he is doing and knows his subject very well
indeed. It will be a big help to all who make use of it . . . Jeff has
put a lot of very useful work into this tome, and I am sure you will
benefit greatly from adding this book to your collection."

—DOUGLAS H. GRESHAM
Author of *Lenten Lands* and *Jack's Life*, coauthor of
The Narnian Cookbook, actor, writer, film and record
producer, radio host, dairy farmer, mechanic, public speaker, and loving stepson of C. S. Lewis

"In this introduction to C. S. Lewis, you will meet Lewis's friends,
learn what he read, and find out why he chose a lion named Aslan
to rule over Narnia. Voth provides a (wardrobe?) door to consider
Lewis's world. The approach is personal, with firsthand accounts
of those who knew Lewis, and full of devotional warmth. You will
certainly discover new reasons for why we love that influential
British scholar."

—BETHANY SOLLEREDER
Research Fellow, Laudato Si' Research Institute, Campion
Hall, University of Oxford, and former Warden of the Kilns

"Each of the seven reasons presented in *Why Lewis?* is extremely
convincing. If just one of them could take the reader one step
closer to the fascinating world of Lewis, the person will see the
door to the life-changing truth right before him or her. This has
been the author's vocation, and he does it brilliantly, as this book
well demonstrates."

—WONSUK MA
Dean and Distinguished Professor of Global Christianity,
College of Theology & Ministry, Oral Roberts University

"Professor Voth does Lewis readers a wonderful service. In *Why Lewis?* he offers a primer to those interested in taking their first steps into the deep, life-giving pools of Lewis's writing. At the same time, he reminds the longtime Lewis explorer of why he first drew them in. And, like Lewis, Voth provides a starting point to further explore other important writers and ideas."

—STEVEN ELMORE
President, C. S. Lewis Foundation, Redlands, California

Why Lewis?

Why Lewis?

Seven Reasons Why C. S. Lewis
is the Second Most Influential Author
in Modern Christian History

Jeff Voth

RESOURCE *Publications* · Eugene, Oregon

WHY LEWIS?
Seven Reasons Why C. S. Lewis is the Second Most Influential Author in
Modern Christian History

Resource Publications
An Imprint of Wipf and Stock Publishers
199 W. 8th Ave., Suite 3
Eugene, OR 97401

www.wipfandstock.com

PAPERBACK ISBN: 978-1-6667-1107-3
HARDCOVER ISBN: 978-1-6667-1108-0
EBOOK ISBN: 978-1-6667-1109-7

08/09/21

Contents

Preface

IN JUNE 2018, I would be afforded the opportunity of a lifetime: a three-week stay at The Kilns in Headington Quarry, England. Yes, miracles do happen, and regular guys like me get to share the space where C. S. Lewis once lived and breathed. Thanks to the gracious people at the C. S. Lewis Foundation, I was given the opportunity to live and study at The Kilns for almost a month. I was forever changed by living in Christian community in the house where Lewis penned many of the classics that have blessed and challenged countless numbers of pilgrims over six decades. Imaginations have been piqued, intellects stimulated, and lives greatly encouraged by what happened there. I know mine has been.

This simple little book was one of the products of my time at The Kilns. It is a Lewis primer, if you will. Something to get you thinking. It is not very deep, nor is it intended to be. It is designed to stimulate your thinking about Lewis and the things that he wrote about, thought about, and stood for, and then animate you to go and think, write, and stand for some things yourself. I will provide footnotes and references to assist the budding Lewis scholar in deeper study, and introduce lists of books and sources that may be new to you. For those who have read everything written under the sun about Lewis, I might be able to offer a couple of first-hand anecdotes of my interactions with some primary sources to the Lewis legacy that will make you smile or give you some new insight or perspective.

The Kilns was named for the two large red brick ovens that used to stand on the property for the purpose of forming and firing bricks that would be building blocks for houses and buildings in Oxford and the surrounding regions. It's funny that that is what Lewis would do there—make bricks. He created images and thought patterns that would be fired and cooked in classrooms, the marketplace, around dinner tables, in pubs, churches, prisons, prayer closets, story times, and people's personal and private studies. What he did at The Kilns would help build better, smarter, more vibrant, imaginative followers of Jesus. What he did there at The Kilns invites us to dream and to think and to allow our dreaming and our thinking to intersect and explode into world-changing, life-giving ideas and lives.

Over the course of my stay at The Kilns, there were some guests who would come for scheduled guided tours, but many would literally pop out from behind the hedgerow to look in amazement at the red brick house that they had seen in pictures or read about in Lewis's biographies. Popping out from the hedgerow were university presidents, deans, scholars, and scores of other regular folks who just wanted to catch a glimpse of The Kilns. But, out of all of the scheduled and chance meetings that occurred, there were two that have left indelible marks upon me.

The first meeting had to do with the room in which I had been assigned to live, the Doug Gresham Room. Doug Gresham is the son of Lewis's wife, Joy. He was eight years old when he and his brother (David[1]), along with their mother (Joy) moved into The Kilns. I had seen pictures and videos of him, so I knew what he looked and sounded like. I'm sure you can imagine that when I came walking back from shopping for groceries on my first afternoon as a resident and saw someone peering in my window who looked and sounded very much like Doug Gresham, I was a bit surprised. Like pictures I had seen, the man at my window was sporting the characteristic hat, riding boots, khakis, and turtleneck. Could it be, I wondered? I must admit that my initial surprise turned to flummoxed amazement when the man spun around, and it was the one

---

1. David Gresham is Doug's older brother, but he has never had a desire to be involved or engaged with the Lewis legacy or his family. His wishes will be respected in this work as well.

and only Doug Gresham. I was speechless. Doug, never speechless and always quick with a phrase, quipped, "I hear you're staying in my room." I responded, "Well, it's mine now, but you're welcome to come in and have a tour if you'd like." We laughed, he graciously posed for a couple of pictures, then shot a short video reenacting our meeting, so that people would actually believe me. After that we went inside, and I was privileged to get some of his firsthand insights about his old home, insights that gave me a personal perspective from which I will glean for many years to come.

The second meeting that is indelibly etched into my mind was my encounter with the delightful and classy gentleman, Walter Hooper. Walter was a young scholar when Lewis reached out to him in 1962, asking him to come to Oxford and act as his secretary as Lewis had been very sick and his brother Warnie, who had taken care of secretarial duties for many years, was away. Not being known for tidiness, Lewis needed someone to come and bring some semblance of order to his many manuscripts, files, letters, books, and papers that had been stacked and piled all over the place in no particular order for many years. Thankfully, Walter said yes, because Lewis would die very soon thereafter, and it is quite possible that we would have had far fewer of his books, letters, and valuable manuscripts had Walter not been there. In a later chapter, I will give a more detailed account about Walter's contributions to Lewis's literary legacy as a result of his relatively short, stay at The Kilns.

My meeting Walter happened to be in conjunction with a group that had scheduled a question-and-answer session with him after their tour of The Kilns. I was asked by the leader of the group if I would stay outside of the library, in the yard, and assist Walter in getting into the house. Of course I said yes, then chuckled to myself about the blessing that it would be to meet yet another living witness to the Lewis legacy. I wondered what he would be like. How tall was he? Would he have an accent? I didn't have to wait long as the English, wood-sided taxi pulled into the drive after my being outside for only a couple of minutes. Out of the taxi jumped a young man of about thirty years old, whom I assumed was not

Walter. He ran to the other side of the taxi, opened the door and helped out a dapper looking gentleman, wearing wire-rimmed glasses, a green tweed jacket, and a royal blue shirt with a red tie. He was using a redwood cane and only needed a bit of help.

As I moved towards Walter and his friend, I gave the typical pleasantry, "How are you sir?" to which he gave the atypical response, "Better now that I've seen you." He then grabbed my hand, as I had reached for him and continued, "And I wish that I looked as good as you sir. What brings you to The Kilns? Have you seen Jack yet?" Jack is the name used by Lewis's closest friends and family. He had chosen it for himself as a young boy, due to the fact that he did not like his given name, Clive. I will use both names for him throughout this book.

Now I really don't think that he was speaking about a ghost, nor do I think that he was out of his mind, as he would prove his mental agility by answering questions and telling detailed stories for the next hour and a half. I do however believe that he probably meant to ask, "Have you seen Jack's house?" But whether it was a Freudian slip, or a slip of the tongue, Walter's question was powerful. I certainly don't believe that Jack's spirit is walking through that place, but I must say that his remembrance certainly is. So, yes Walter, I saw Jack. I saw him as I remembered. As I remembered a lion and a warrior mouse. As I remembered *Mere Christianity*, *A Grief Observed*, and the green lady of *Perelandra*. I saw and remembered many things there at The Kilns. But ultimately, I saw Jesus. So as I saw Jack and Jesus through those remembrances, I was reminded that those are the kinds of remembrances that are the best, holy and life-giving ones. I had too many of them during my stay at The Kilns to count.

Many thanks to the C. S. Lewis Foundation, Jack, Doug, Walter, and Jesus.

Jeff Voth
C. S. Lewis Foundation Resident Scholar,
at the Kilns, Headington Quarry
June 6–June 27, 2018

Introduction

As Henry L. Carrigan, Jr. puts it in *Publishers Weekly*,
"While Huxley is now largely forgotten and Kennedy
remains a symbol of lost promise, Lewis lives on
through his novels, stories, essays, and autobiographical
works." While I think that oversimplifies Kennedy and
underestimates Huxley, the underlying point is worth
considering: In one of the great ironies of history, Lewis
at his death received less attention than Huxley, and far
less than Kennedy. But it may be true that Lewis's ideas
claim the most lasting influence, both on the Christian
tradition and on the Western culture beyond.[1]

AARON CLINE HANBURY,
commenting in his article in *The Atlantic* concerning the
deaths and legacies of John F. Kennedy, Aldous Huxley,
and C. S. Lewis, who all died on November 22, 1963.

IT HAS BEEN SAID that next to the biblical writers, the most quoted person in American pulpits, churches, and educational institutions, hands down, is C. S. Lewis. I quote him, you quote him, your pastor quotes him, your teachers and professors quote him, and they do so without even thinking about it. He has become such

1. Hanbury, "Why C. S. Lewis Never Goes Out of Style."

a part of the speaking and thinking rhythm of those of us in the West, that without him, well . . . who would we quote? Peter Kreeft sums it up quite nicely, "(Lewis) is read with enormous affection and loyalty by a wide and diversified audience today. . . . In fact, more of his books are sold today than those of any other Christian writer in history."[2]

Have you ever wondered why? I have.

Why is it that this North-Irish-born transplant to Oxford has become so popular that five and a half decades after his death we are still quoting him on a daily or at least weekly basis? Was he that good? How is it that he was able to strike a chord that resonates in our heads and our hearts in a way that no one else has been able to accomplish? Was it his ability to tell a story? Or was it that he could break down lofty, philosophical arguments without condescension in such a way that those of us who were significantly less smart might understand? Whatever the reasons, and there seem to be many, I think his crazy popularity and vast impact merit a book that aims to start a conversation around the simple question, "Why Lewis?"

And while I realize that there is no way that we will ever come close to arriving at an exhaustive, final conclusion, the mere (pun intended and see what I mean?) fact that his presence is so pervasive demands a response. So, in the next few chapters, I am going to provide my personal list of reasons and attempt to establish a cumulative case. By doing this, I hope to stimulate you to come up with reasons of your own and together we might explore (in my not-so-humble opinion), seven reasons why I think that C. S. Lewis is the second-most-influential writer in modern Christian history.

2. Kreeft, "Lewis and the Two Roads," 354.

Reason #1

Because the Numbers Don't Lie

BEFORE LAUNCHING INTO REASON #1, I probably need to answer the question that you have been asking yourself since reading the subtitle of this book or the last statement of the previous section, that I would be presenting " seven reasons why I think that C. S. Lewis is the second-most-influential writer in modern Christian history." This undoubtedly begs the question: "If Lewis is number 2, then who's number 1?" That's easy . . . God (via the writers of the Bible). As of 2015, *The Guinness Book of World Records* holds that The Bible is in a category all its own at five billion estimated copies sold in modern history.[1]

While Lewis's books haven't sold close to the Bible's numbers, they do continue to sell, influence, and impact reader after reader, life after life, mind after mind, year after year. The bottom line is that it is hard to argue with success. So, my reason #1 is *because the numbers don't lie*. Young and old alike read Lewis's books. Malleable minds, as well as the ones that have been set in their ways for quite some time, are both affected. And he affects readers through the vehicles of fiction and nonfiction as well. Personally, as a writer of primarily nonfiction books, I understand how difficult and uncommon this is to accomplish. I have currently been working on a piece of fiction that has taken me over seven years, and I am still not even close to getting it published. Lewis was an anomaly in this regard.

1. "Best-selling Book," in Glenday, *Guinness Book.*

Why Lewis?

While his friend J. R. R. Tolkien was arguably a better writer of fiction than was Lewis, as overall sales of Tolkien's books might show, he (Tolkien) didn't write much prose that has had the lasting, broad impact that Lewis's writing has had. By this I mean, when was the last time that you started a phrase with, "Tolkien said in *The Silmarillion* that . . ."[2] But it may have been as recently as this morning that you interjected the phrase, "Lewis said in *Mere Christianity*" or one of my personal go-to statements is "Aslan is on the move." The references just go on and on and, as I said before, often it is done without the speaker even thinking about it. Lewis's broad "cross-genre" appeal seems to be unparalleled, and while some may argue that I am exaggerating, maybe it's best to let the numbers speak for themselves.

Stats

In addition to Lewis's hundreds of essays and short writings, his major works have impacted three primary streams of literature: scholarly works, apologetics, and fiction. And as I have already stated, even those who don't ascribe to his Christian faith have at least a general knowledge of him, being able to easily recall that he was the "guy who wrote *The Chronicles of Narnia*." In 2000, *Christianity Today* asked one hundred contributors and church leaders to nominate their top ten most impactful books of the twentieth century. Out of the millions of potential books and authors that qualified for the list, C. S. Lewis was by far the most popular author and *Mere Christianity* was, hands down, the number 1 book. In fact, the article announcing the results stated, "Indeed, we could have included even more of Lewis's works, but finally we had to say, 'Enough is enough; give some other authors a chance.'"[3]

However, since this is a book about Lewis's impact, I am not going to give other authors a chance, unless it is to show how their

---

2. *The Silmarillion*, also known as *Translations from the Elvish* (a five-part collection of J. R. R. Tolkien's works that were edited and published posthumously by his son Christopher Tolkien and fantasy writer Guy Gavriel Kay).

3. "Books of the Century."

impact is (in my not-so-humble opinion) far lesser than Lewis's. So, sit back, relax, and be regaled with some noteworthy stats.

1. Lewis's books have been translated into more than forty languages and have sold millions of copies. The seven books that make up *The Chronicles of Narnia*, first published between 1950 and 1956, have sold the most—estimated at 150 million copies—and have been popularized on stage, TV, radio, and the movies.[4]

2. As of 2013, *Mere Christianity* had sold eighteen million copies and continues to sell about one million copies per year.[5]

3. It is estimated that annual sales of Lewis's books range as high as six million copies.[6]

4. In all, Lewis edited or authored 110 books, and there are more than 300 books that discuss him and his work, with new ones published every year, many as bestsellers.[7]

5. The combined box office sales for the three Narnia films so far total $1.5 billion, and the film series is the twenty-fourth highest grossing of all time.[8]

6. Until J. K. Rowling published the Harry Potter series, the seven volumes of Lewis's *The Chronicles of Narnia* book series were the most influential children's books in the world, voted so by successive polls of parents, librarians, and teachers, and demonstrated by their sales. And, the Harry Potter books haven't cut into Narnia's market. Indeed, they've greatly expanded it as sales of the Narniad have increased by 20 percent during this time.[9]

4. Theroux, "Why C. S. Lewis Is as Influential as Ever."
5. Hanbury, "Why C. S. Lewis Never Goes Out of Style."
6. Theroux, "Why C. S. Lewis Is as Influential as Ever."
7. Theroux, "Why C. S. Lewis Is as Influential as Ever."
8. Theroux, "Why C. S. Lewis Is as Influential as Ever."
9. Theroux, "Why C. S. Lewis Is as Influential as Ever."

7. Today, there are also over 300 C. S. Lewis Societies around the world, and a C. S. Lewis College is in the works in Massachusetts.[10]

8. In November 2013, fifty years after his death, to celebrate and acknowledge his achievements as a writer, officials of Westminster Abbey honored Lewis with a memorial stone in the prestigious Poets' Corner alongside literary figures such as Geoffrey Chaucer and Charles Dickens.[11]

It could be argued that this list of statistics might continue, at least a bit longer, but I think my point has been made. Whether one is a fan or not, Lewis's influence cannot and should not be ignored. Therefore, let's forge ahead toward reason #2 in my cumulative case and meet those people who were engaged with Lewis in the warp and woof of his life and were ultimately involved in some form or fashion with his development into the towering figure that has cast such a huge shadow in so many arenas.

10. Theroux, "Why C. S. Lewis Is as Influential as Ever."
11. Hanbury, "Why C. S. Lewis Never Goes Out of Style."

Reason #2

Because His Inner Circle Is Legendary

AESOP SAID THAT "A man is known by the company he keeps." Another way to say this might be that you can know a man better by knowing his "inner circle," those with whom he was/is closest. This ancient truth may be a good thing or a bad one, depending on the company or circle being referenced. In Lewis's case, the circle included modern-day literary giants, beloved family members, professorial colleagues, deceased tutors, persons with whom he was enamored, and, as hard as it may be to believe, an outspoken legendary critic who would engage him in both public and private debate. Whatever the case, in order to gain more insight into why I make such an audacious claim regarding Lewis's impact upon modern history, one must be introduced to the company he kept. So, reason #2 in my cumulative case for Lewis's incomparable influence is *because his inner circle is legendary.*

His Mentor: George MacDonald

I have never concealed the fact that I regard George MacDonald as my master; indeed, I fancy I have never written a book in which I did not quote from him.[1]

C. S. LEWIS

1. Lewis, "Preface," xxxvii.

Why Lewis?

Hardly any other writer who seems to be closer, or more
continuously close, to the Spirit of Christ Himself.[2]

C. S. LEWIS

While it is true that Lewis and MacDonald were alive briefly during the same time period and in the same geographical proximity,
Belfast and Aberdeen respectively, the fact that MacDonald died
on September 18, 1905, when Lewis was only seven years old pre-
cluded them from having an actual physical relationship. However,
as attested to by the previous quote, MacDonald's impact on Lewis's
mind and spirit were foundational. Undeniably, the relationships
Lewis would have with his contemporaries, especially the Inklings
(to be discussed later in this chapter) would prove to be extremely
important on many levels, but MacDonald's influence seems to
have been unparalleled, especially in Lewis's mind, by empowering
him to fully engage his imagination. Lewis lists MacDonald's *Phantastes* as number 1 on his list of books that influenced him most
holistically as a person. Suffice it to say that whether or not one
ends up being the adoring fan Lewis was, in order to understand
Lewis more fully, one should read some of MacDonald's works.[3]

The Inklings

After MacDonald, undoubtedly the most renowned collective
group of influencers upon Lewis's life, were the Inklings. This
group was established for the purpose of engaging in debate, cri-
tique, and healthy conversation pertaining to various works being
presented by some of the members. In his seminal book entitled
*The Inklings: C. S. Lewis, J. R. R. Tolkien, Charles Williams and Their
Friends*, Humphrey Carpenter defines them as "a group of friends,
many of them Oxford dons, who referred to themselves informally
and half jestingly as 'The Inklings' . . . who owed their existence

2. Lewis, "Preface," xxxvii.

3. A suggested reading list of MacDonald's work is included in the
Appendix.

almost entirely to [Lewis]."[4] Their membership consisted primarily of Lewis, J. R. R. Tolkien, Charles Williams, Warren "Warnie" Lewis, Owen Barfield, Hugo Dyson, Nevill Coghill, Colin Hardie, R. E. "Humphrey" Havard, and Christopher Tolkien. However, throughout the years there would ultimately be nineteen men who would attend Inkling meetings, both regularly and sporadically,[5] with some combination of the aforementioned being the most consistent members.

Inkling meetings took place between 1933 and 1963 in Lewis's rooms at Oxford, in the Rabbit Room at The Eagle and Child pub (also known as The Bird and Baby)—or, after a squabble with the owner of "The Bird"—across the street at The Lamb & Flag. Typically, meetings would commence with Lewis saying, "Well, has nobody got anything to read us?"[6] and invariably someone would have something. And if walls could speak, they would speak of some very, very substantive and influential somethings that were read and discussed in one of those smoky mythical little pubs on Thursday evenings. They would have heard Lewis read parts of such works as *Out of the Silent Planet*, *The Great Divorce*, *Miracles*, *The Screwtape Letters*, and *The Lion, the Witch and the Wardrobe*.[7] Tolkien would bring chapters from *The Hobbit*, *The Lord of the Rings*, and some of his poetry. Charles Williams, Warnie, Owen Barfield, and the others would bring their works as well. But, despite the fact that the Inklings had among their fraternity some of the most prolific and impactful writers in modern history, none would impact Lewis more, nor be closer to him in life and death, than his beloved brother Warnie.

4. Carpenter, *Inklings*, ix.
5. Glyer, "C. S. Lewis."
6. Glyer, "C. S. Lewis."
7. McGrath, *C. S. Lewis*, 175–81.

His Brother: Warnie

He was my dearest and closest friend.[8]

C. S. LEWIS

Warren Hamilton "Warnie" Lewis, the older brother of C. S. Lewis, was born on June 16, 1895. Due to the untimely death of their mother, Flora Hamilton Lewis, on August 23, 1908, and relational estrangement from their father, who simply couldn't handle Flora's death, the boys grew to be not only the closest of brothers, but the deepest of friends. It would be a relationship that even death could not separate, as Warnie's casket would eventually be laid to rest on top of Jack's on April 9, 1973, in the cemetery at Holy Trinity Church, Headington Quarry, Oxford.

In life, the brothers' early boyhood years in Northern Ireland were marked by much reading, exploration, and the creation of imaginary worlds where talking animals built advanced civilizations while engaging in epic battles. But eventually those idyllic times of reading, dreaming, exploring, and world-creating would be punctuated by periods of both short and, ultimately, lengthy separation. However, despite being separated by Warnie attending boarding school, Jack going to university, or both serving in World War I, the brothers remained deeply bound. Consistent letters, telegraphs, and holiday celebrations ensured that their lives remained intertwined.

Ultimately, after being wounded in World War I, Jack returned to Oxford and began living with the family of a fallen army comrade, Paddy Moore. Jack and Paddy had become close friends while in basic training, making a pact that should one of them be killed, the survivor would take care of the other's parents. Unfortunately Moore was killed. Jack, honoring his word, moved in with and cared for Paddy's mother, Mrs. Janie Moore, and her daughter Maureen. The threesome bounced around and lived in different rented accommodations in Oxford from 1921 to 1930.

8. "C. S. Lewis: A Gallery of Family and Friends."

Then, in October 1930, Mrs. Moore, Jack, and Warnie (home on leave from the army), purchased a property together. The home was called "The Kilns," due to two large brick kiln ovens that still sat on the property. In 1932, Warnie retired from the military and joined Jack and the Moores full-time. The brothers were reunited.

Between 1929 and 1931, Jack and Warnie, each in their own way, arrived at a place where they believed that Christianity was the truest faith. While J. R. R. Tolkien, Owen Barfield, and Hugo Dyson were instrumental in wrestling Jack to the faith, Warnie seems to have arrived there on his own.[9] By 1933, the fraternal brothers were now brothers in Christ. During this period, the two would begin to embark upon their beloved and legendary walking tours, where they would traverse the English countryside conversing and debating about theology, philosophy, literature, beer, politics, and anything and everything in between.[10]

It is during this period when Warnie would become Jack's secretary, returning letters, editing books, and typing scripts. Jack, neither friend nor fan of the typewriter, welcomed Warnie's abilities and willingness to engage in these all-important activities. Despite his life-long battle with alcoholism, Warnie endeavored to be as committed to his brother as possible and was very helpful during periods of sobriety. His love for Jack was deep, and he did much good work returning Jack's growing mountain of fan letters. He also accompanied Jack on social functions and helped him manage his ever-tightening calendar of events. In fact, it is Warnie who would ultimately introduce Jack to his future wife, Joy Davidman Gresham, as a result of his reading and discussing some of her thought-provoking fan letters with Jack.

Gresham, a single, separated American woman, who was a former atheist, with two sons had become an adoring Lewis fan.[11]

9. Carpenter, *Inklings*, 52.

10. While Warnie was not the literary force that Jack was, he would ultimately publish at least seven works pertaining to seventeenth century French history, some of which were most certainly discussed at the Inklings meetings.

11. Joy Davidman Gresham, her son Douglas, and their relationships with Jack will be discussed in greater detail later in this chapter.

Mere Christianity had had a profound impact upon her, leading her to a real, logical, and vibrant faith in Jesus. She and Jack (with Warnie in tow the first couple of times) would eventually meet and engage in a somewhat secretive relationship and, ultimately, marry. Unfortunately, their time together would be short, spending only a few cancer-marred yet beautiful years together. Doug Gresham, Joy's son, aptly reflects upon the deep fraternal bond between the two Lewis brothers as he observed Warnie minister to his mother, during one of her bouts with terminal cancer: "Warnie supported Jack all through this terrible time; he consoled his brother when Jack's sorrow became too much for him, he worked ever harder on Jack's correspondence to try to give Jack more time to be with Mother. When Jack had to be away, Warnie would sit for hours with Mother, talking or reading to her. Whenever a crisis arose, Warnie would always be there, supportive, but never intrusive."[12]

The relationship between the brothers seems to have been so deep that when Jack passed away, Warnie was never able to fully recover. Gresham writes, "I cannot remember ever seeing him completely sober after Jack's death . . . and I never again met the charming gentle old Warnie whom I had loved and respected."[13] Sadly, after ten years of lonely, mostly intoxicated grief, on April 9, 1973, Warnie passed away, laid to rest in peace for eternity with his beloved brother and dearest friend, Jack. The following phrase Warnie placed upon Jack's headstone would oddly also be his own epitaph. I have included it here, modified slightly, yet fittingly by their friend and stepson Doug Gresham in expression of his own grief at their passings, "Men must endure their going hence, but I wish they had not gone."[14]

12. Gresham, *Lenten Lands*, 75.

13. Gresham, *Lenten Lands*, 191–92.

14. Gresham, *Lenten Lands*, 213. The first portion of this quote, "Men must endure their going hence" is a quote from Shakespeare's *King Lear* that Warnie had inscribed on Jack's grave marker. He did so due to the fact that the quote was on a calendar that hung in his mother's room on the day that she died. Warnie's father held onto that leaf of paper for the rest of his life. I have concluded this section with a quote from *Lenten Lands* where Doug Gresham added his own fitting verbiage in homage to Warnie, Jack, and their going hence.

His Colleague: Tollers

He is a very good man. His published works (both
imaginary & scholarly) ought to fill a shelf by now.[15]

C. S. LEWIS

John Ronald Reuel Tolkien (1892–1973), or "Tollers" as he was
known to Jack, is arguably one of the most important and influential writers of fiction in modern history and quite possibly ever.
His *The Hobbit* and *The Lord of the Rings* book series have impacted
countless numbers of people of all ages. However, it goes without
saying that whenever Tolkien's name is spoken, even if one doesn't
say it, more often than not one will end up thinking about Jack as
well and vice versa. I realize that I may be overstating my case a
bit, but the two had an immense impact upon one another, and
without Tolkien's brilliant defense and presentation of the Christian faith to an atheistic and unbelieving young Jack, the classics
that would flow from Jack's pen might never have made it to paper.

While it is true that they first met at Oxford as colleagues as
early as 1926, their more intimate friendship was initially forged
in 1929 on the anvil of a mutual admiration for Old Icelandic
and Old Norse literature. This admiration was fostered through
a group led by Tolkien called the Kolbitar (Coalbiters). The Coalbiters received their name due to the fact that in order to keep
warm during their meetings in the winter, one had to sit so close to
the fire to get warm that it was as if he were "biting the coals." Ultimately Jack and Tolkien became so enthralled by their interaction
at Coalbiters meetings that their conversations began to extend
long into the night. Those conversations, pertaining primarily to
things Norse, reignited in Jack a deep love for some of the myths
and characters of which he had been so fond as a child. Tales of
dragons, pale skies, courage against the darkness, and vulnerable
gods, especially one called Balder struck him anew in a most powerful way.

15. Lewis, *Collected Letters*, vol. 2, 630.

This new appreciation for old myths and lengthy conversations with Tolkien created a synergy that propelled Jack in 1929 to become not yet a Christian, but a theist. Then, in 1931, while walking with Tolkien and good friend, Hugo Dyson, on Addison's Walk, Jack could no longer resist. Like a sudden burst of wind through the trees, the reality hit him, and he became convinced of the truth of theism and, ultimately, the Christian faith.[16] Tolkien had helped him to see that Christianity was in fact the "True Myth."[17] He would maintain that all of the myths that had captivated him pointed in some form or fashion toward the ultimate and prevailing truth of the Christian one. Jack would recount:

> The heart of Christianity is a myth which is also a fact. The old myth of the Dying God, without ceasing to be myth, comes down from the heaven of legend and the imagination to the earth of history. It happens—at a particular date, in a particular place, followed by definable historical consequences. We pass from a Balder or Osiris, dying nobody knows when or where, to a historical Person crucified (it's all in order) under *Pontius Pilate*. By becoming fact it does not cease to be myth: that is the miracle.[18]

Tolkien and Jack began to walk together as brothers in Christ. They were colleagues, Inklings, and friends. Through the late 1930s their relationship would grow and prove to be mutually stimulating. Inklings meetings were formative and synergistic for both. However, as Jack would describe to friend Arthur Greeves, in his mind, he and Tolkien were friends of a "second class."[19] While he

---

16. It is important to note here that between September 19, 1931, and September 28, 1931, Lewis would arrive at the conclusion that Christianity was true. His time with Tolkien and Dyson on Addison's Walk was where the process started; it culminated in the realization that he was a Christian upon arriving at Whipsnade Zoo. For a detailed explanation of these events, see McGrath, *C. S. Lewis*, 151–59.

17. The "True Myth" is a pivotal concept in Lewis's salvation and will be discussed at length in chapter 6.

18. Lewis, *Weight of Glory*, 41.

19. Carpenter, *Inklings*, 33.

didn't use this term in a demeaning context, it may have set the stage for two events that one would not necessarily share with a second class friend, and these two events would have an adverse effect upon them ever becoming friends of the first class. The first event would be the sudden arrival of author, poet, lecturer, and eventual Inkling, Charles Williams, in 1936. The second was Jack's marriage to Joy Gresham, an event that went unannounced to Tolkien. It seems that these two happenings drove a wedge between the two men, at least in Tolkien's mind. He says as much in a letter to one of his children:

> I am sorry that I have not answered your letters sooner; but Jack Lewis's death on the 22nd has preoccupied me. It is also involving me in some correspondence, as many people still regard me as one of his intimates. Alas! that ceased to be some 10 years ago. We were separated first by the sudden apparition of Charles Williams, and then by his marriage. But we owed each a great debt to the other, and that tie, with the deep affection that it begot, remained. He was a great man of whom the cold-blooded official obituaries have only scraped the surface.[20]

While much has been written about and many have pondered the relationship between Jack and Tolkien, it cannot be denied that the two had a deep love for one another. Without Tolkien in his life, Jack could have remained separated from Christ for many more years and, possibly, eternally. It is undeniable that he was eternally grateful. And without Jack in Tolkien's life, *The Hobbit* and *The Lord of the Rings* may have never been more than myths living only in Tolkien's mind. It would be unfair to expect that through the warp and woof of the lives of two such powerful and talented men, that some stresses and strains might not follow. Lewis scholar and biographer Colin Duriez summarizes these sentiments nicely:

> The friendship between Tolkien and Lewis lasted from soon after their first meeting in 1926 until Lewis' death in 1963. Like all friendships, especially those lasting over such an extended period, there were ups

20. Carpenter, *Inklings*, 252.

and downs. With Lewis and Tolkien, a distinct cooling took place in the final years, though the similarities that united them were always stronger than the differences that separated them.[21]

"The Apparition": Charles Williams

In appearance he was tall, slim and straight as a boy, though grey-haired. His face we thought ugly . . . but the moment he spoke it became . . . like the face of an angel—not a feminine angel in the debased tradition of some religious art, but a masculine angel, a spirit burning with intelligence and charity. . . . No man whom I have known was at the same time less affected and more flamboyant in his manners: and also more playful. . . . He threw down all his barriers without even implying that you should lower yours.[22]

C. S. LEWIS

An apparition (a sudden, ghost-like appearance) to one man, might be perceived as an angel by another. That was obviously the case when it came to the opinions of Tolkien and Jack regarding the sudden appearance of Charles Walter Stansby Williams into Jack's life and therefore into the lives of those around him. While being called an "apparition" by Tolkien wasn't necessarily derogatory in and of itself, it certainly wasn't meant as a compliment either. It was obviously used by Tolkien to describe why he felt that he and Jack had fallen out of their once intimate friendship. Whatever the case may be, Jack's regard for Williams was of the highest order, and it came about rather quickly; so to be fair, Tolkien's apparition remark seems appropriate.

Before bursting onto the scene, Williams worked as a proof-reader and editor at Oxford Press (London), starting work there in

21. Duriez, *Tolkien and C. S. Lewis*, x.

22. Lewis, *Essays Presented to Charles Williams*, vi–vii.

1908. During that time, he also became immersed in writing poetry, plays, novels, biographies, and literary criticisms, which achieved modest success. His works were predominantly focused on deeply spiritual issues, especially black and white magic, the occult, and Rosicrucianism.[23] His greatest success, however, was as a lecturer, where he became very popular, especially with female students.

Jack was personally introduced to Williams and his work by friend and fellow Inkling, Nevill Coghill. The introduction was through a book written by Williams in 1931, entitled *The Place of the Lion*, and it is fair to say that Jack was smitten by it. He expresses his sentiments in a letter to his friend Arthur Greeves:

> I have just read what I think a really great book, *The Place of the Lion*, by Charles Williams. . . . It is not only a most exciting fantasy, but a deeply religious and (unobtrusively) a profoundly learned book. . . . I have learned more than I ever knew yet about humility. In fact, it has been a big experience. Do get it, and don't mind if you don't understand everything the first time. It deserves reading over and over again.[24]

Needless to say, as a result of Lewis's strong feelings for the book, he reached out to Williams by letter in 1936, expressing his fondness for it. Williams responded to Lewis's overture, and the two began to exchange letters, expressing their mutual admiration for one another's writings. Then, as fate would have it, due to World War II, Oxford Press relocated Williams to their office in Oxford in 1939, availing Jack and him the opportunity to connect on a regular basis, especially through weekly Inkling meetings. He, more than any of the other Inklings, would ultimately have the most profound and positive impact upon Jack. In fact, biographer and friend to both men, George Sayer, would recount:

23. Rosicrucianism is the study of metaphysical, mystical, and alchemical lore.

24. Lewis, *Letters of C. S. Lewis to Arthur Greeves*, 479. Jack's letters to Greeves span fifty years as Greeves was undoubtedly a close and trusted confidant. A case could be made that next to his brother Warnie, he was his most trusted friend. For the purposes of this book, however, I have chosen to focus upon his more famous and well-known friends.

> Jack was devoted to all his friends, but he loved Wil-
> liams the most. Their friendship perfectly fulfilled the
> ideals that Jack would later describe in *The Four Loves*.
> They shared a common purpose and, vision, romanti-
> cism and Christianity, and a love of both orthodoxy and
> wild speculation.[25]

The above mentioned "wild speculation" would lend itself to far-ranging ideas, ones that would run the gamut of philosophy, religion, poetry, and literature. One such idea purported by Williams that intrigued Jack deeply was his theory of "substitution." This theory held that one could offer to take on suffering for the welfare of another. Many years later, Jack's own wife, Joy, was stricken with cancer. Of course, Jack prayed desperately for her to be healed, and for a while she was. During the same time, however, Jack got sick and felt immense pain in his own body. He couldn't help but think that Williams's theory of substitution may have been occurring between Joy and him.

The mutual influence of Lewis and Williams upon one another was undeniable. In Williams, Jack's passion for the poetry of Wordsworth and Milton was equaled, and perhaps his ability and affinity for quoting it may have been surpassed. The two were known to recite long passages by memory to each other and anyone else in earshot. Numerous examples of Williams's impact upon Jack's writing might be found, especially in the last book of *The Space Trilogy*, *That Hideous Strength*. In it, Williams's vision of a world filled with psychological and cosmic experiences of evil is embodied in the perverted Belbury scientists who rely heavily upon black magic. The presence of the legendary Arthurian wizard Merlin may undoubtedly be attributed to Williams's deep love for Arthurian poetry and lore.

Jack's influence upon Williams's literary works may not be as obvious, due to the fact that Williams was quite simply not as gifted as Jack at conveying his ideas to such a broad audience. However, because of Jack's broad appeal, and an undying public interest in those who influenced him, many have sought out the

---

25. Sayer, *Jack*, 295.

work of Williams and been stimulated by it. It cannot be denied that Jack loved Williams's writings as much or more than anyone else and encouraged his friends, students, and colleagues to engage in them wholeheartedly. Jack's love and appreciation for Williams's entire body of work went far beyond talking of him and writing about him to his friends and colleagues. He sincerely felt that Williams needed to be recognized officially by the Academy. Therefore, Jack arranged for him to receive an honorary master's degree from Oxford (for Williams had no earned degree); Lewis then pushed to get him an appointment as a Professor of Poetry. Alas, despite Lewis's reputation and Williams's popularity as a lecturer, there would be no official faculty appointment.

When it became apparent to Williams that he would not receive the appointment, he resolved to move back to London in May 1945. Learning of this, Jack organized and prompted six of the Inklings (Dorothy Sayer, Warnie, Owen Barfield, Gervase Mathew, Tolkien, and Jack) to write a series of essays in his honor. Williams would never see the essays, however, as he became very ill and died suddenly on May 15, 1945. The book *Essays Presented to Charles Williams* would be completed in his honor posthumously in 1947. While all of the essays were heartfelt and substantive, Tolkien's "On Fairy Stories" and Jack's "On Stories" are classics.

Undoubtedly, Williams's death left a huge hole in Jack's life. Could it ever be filled? Would it ever be filled? George Sayer answers these questions:

> . . . feelings of Williams's presence faded slowly, but they often recurred later in life, especially on the anniversary of his death. It was not until he met Joy Davidman Gresham, the woman that he would later marry, that he found anyone to take Williams's place in his heart.[26]

26. Sayer, *Jack*, 292.

His Beloved and Her Sons: The Greshams
(Joy and Doug)

I could see that Jack and Mother had something
very special and very beautiful . . . Jack and
Mother simply belonged together.[27]

DOUGLAS GRESHAM

A Fan Letter

Had it not been for Jack's dogged commitment that every piece of mail he received be returned, the hole left in his heart by the death of Charles Williams might never have been filled, and the beautiful and special togetherness expressed in the above quote from Doug Gresham would have never occurred either. While many of Jack's growing number of fan letters contained the typical "thank you" verbiage, Joy Davidman Gresham's initial letter stood out. It was heartfelt and witty. Her faith in Christ had been stimulated by Jack's writings, and for that she was thankful. Her letter arrived at The Kilns in January 1950, and both Jack and Warnie found it so well written and amusing that it prompted Jack to write a personal response. While he was committed to seeing that all of his fan letters were answered, Jack was simply not able to respond to all of them himself, so Warnie helped by reading and responding to many of them. Jack's heartfelt response to Joy only intensified her feelings about him and his work, so she set out upon a course to meet him.

At this point in regards to the facts concerning the relationship that ensued between Jack and Joy, I must add that much has been written by many able and fair biographers, and some who are not so fair and able.[28] In my own personal study, I have found that there are some irrefutable facts and dates related to the fast-paced,

27. Gresham, *Lenten Lands*, 89.

28. Here is a list of recommended biographies that chronicle the events pertaining to the relationship between Jack and Joy: Gresham, *Lenten Lands*; Sayer, *Jack*; Dorsett, *And God Came In*; and Green and Hooper, *C. S. Lewis*.

short-lived, yet enduringly beautiful relationship between Jack and Joy, and they are as follows:

1. In 1952, Joy traveled to London to visit a pen pal with whom she had exchanged letters. She reached out to Jack during the visit, asking for advice about her failing marriage as well as some insights regarding a book that she was writing on a practical application of the Ten Commandments that was entitled *Smoke on the Mountain*.

2. Jack invited Joy to the Eastgate Hotel for lunch and was "astonished by 'Her mind was lithe and quick and muscular as a leopard.'"[29]

3. In January 1953, Joy and her sons came to The Kilns for a visit after her marriage had ended.

4. In 1955, Joy moved to Oxford, not far from The Kilns.

5. In 1955, Joy's book *Smoke on the Mountain* was published, with a foreword by Jack.

6. On April 23, 1956, Joy and Jack were married in a civil ceremony to allow her and her boys to stay in Oxford and prevent them from being deported to the United States. She and the boys did not immediately move into The Kilns after the civil ceremony.

7. In November 1956, Joy went to the hospital and was diagnosed with cancer.

8. On March 21, 1957, Joy and Jack were married by a priest in her hospital room. The priest laid hands on her and prayed for healing. She was moved to The Kilns to recover.

9. As of November 5, 1958, Warnie wrote in his diary that Joy had miraculously recovered.[30]

10. Joy was diagnosed with cancer again in October 1959.

11. Jack took Joy on her dream vacation to Greece in Spring 1960.

29. Carpenter, *Inklings*, 237.
30. Carpenter, *Inklings*, 241.

12. Helen Joy Davidman Gresham Lewis died on July 13, 1960.

Some have questioned Joy's motives and methods in meeting and ultimately marrying Jack. Others guess, ponder, gossip, and try and fill in the details and decide for themselves. I have found that when one is dealing with historical events, it is valuable to have personal, primary source interviews. In the case of Jack and Joy, my personal opinion is that Doug Gresham's account in *Lenten Lands* is personal, primary, and extremely valuable, as he was actually there during the events in question.

The Impact of Joy

One of the major themes in Jack's life was joy. The German term he used to describe it was *Sehnsucht,* or longing. He says that it was present in his childhood and ultimately throughout his adult life as well. On one occasion he described it like this:

> All joy reminds. It is never a possession, always a desire for something longer ago, further away, or still "about to be."[31]

On another occasion, he described joy like this:

> In this world, everything is upside down. That which, if it could be prolonged here, would be a truancy, is likest that which in a better country is the End of ends. Joy is the serious business of heaven.[32]

So, a double entendre–filled wink from heaven it was when Joy Davidman Gresham came into his life. As seen above, it can't be denied that the relationship between Jack and Joy took place over only a few short years. However, it also can't be denied that their brief love affair inspired not only them as participants, but countless numbers of bystanders and observers as well. Most will agree that Jack's later works, the ones that came during and post-Joy, possessed an inspiration, clarity, and depth that wasn't as

31. Lewis, *Surprised by Joy*, 78.
32. Lewis, *Letters to Malcolm*, 93.

clearly present in his earlier work. When I read *Till We Have Faces* (1956), *Reflections on the Psalms* (1958), *The Four Loves* (1960), and *A Grief Observed* (1960), I read tales and reflections that ooze with a seasoned pathos, a resolute joy, and a palpable, vibrant, and undying passion. George Sayer, friend to both Jack and Joy, has summed up this classic love story as he remembers:

> In living with Joy, he was being himself. There was no need to posture and play at different roles, except for fun. With her, he was free from self-doubt and introspection. He could speak ideas just as they arose and receive back from her answers or arguments that would stimulate still more interesting ideas in his mind. They were a most blessed and richly gifted pair.[33]

His Secretary: Walter Hooper

> But because of a soft-spoken gentleman who showed up one June day on the doorstep to The Kilns, much has survived and will remain.[34]
>
> DEVIN BROWN

Born in Reedsville, North Carolina, in 1931, Hooper received his master's degree in English in 1958, ultimately becoming an English professor at the University of Kentucky. His first exposure to Jack's work came while reading an introduction Jack had written to a book by J. B. Phillips entitled *Letters to Young Churches*. Hooper says that introduction gripped him in a way that nothing had ever gripped him before. He had never felt someone write with such a voice of faith. "He had the confidence of the Apostles Peter and Paul," Hooper remembers fondly.[35]

---

33. Sayer, *Jack*, 381.

34. Brown, review of *C. S. Lewis and the Church*, 209–11.

35. Hooper, "Life and Writing of C. S. Lewis: Part One."

Why Lewis?

That apostle-like confidence drew him to research Jack's life, work, and faith. That research would spawn a book project, leading him to reach out to Jack and ask if the two might meet as Hooper was, tongue in cheek, planning a trip to study in England. Ultimately, Jack invited Hooper to The Kilns, and the two met on Monday, June 10, 1963 for an interview. Their time together turned out to be so enjoyable that Jack invited Hooper to an Inklings meeting that afternoon, to church at Holy Trinity Church on Sunday, and to yet another visit to The Kilns the next week. Ultimately, these three meetings turned into three meetings per week, culminating in an offer by Jack for Hooper to quit his job and to come to Oxford and be his secretary. Jack had become so severely weakened by a heart attack and failing health that he realized his need for someone of Hooper's nature and abilities to help organize his affairs. Hooper agreed, then went back to Kentucky to quit his job and prepare to move to The Kilns. However, on November 22, 1963, Jack would die about an hour after the late President John F. Kennedy was shot.

In January 1964, Hooper returned to England, this time for good. The reason for his return was in response to Warnie asking him to undertake the editing of the Lewis papers. C. S. Lewis has been Hooper's life's work ever since. He was ordained in 1965 as an Anglican clergyman, and in 1971 became one of the trustees of the Lewis Literary Estate. Warnie, the Greshams, and Jack's friends were elated that someone was prepared to undertake the enormous task of finding and publishing all that remained of Jack's work—and the amount that remained was mountainous. It was so mountainous that Warnie, who was obviously not in a healthy state of mind, had instructed Fred Paxford, the gardener, to burn many items in a bonfire that lasted for three days. However, before he could burn it all, Paxford had reached out to Hooper, inviting him to save as much as he could. Hooper would later write,

> By what seems more than coincidence, I appeared at The Kilns that very day and learned that unless I carried the papers away with me that afternoon they would indeed be

destroyed. There were so many that it took all my strength and energy to carry them back to Keble College.[36]

Since 1964, Hooper has sifted through those materials that he saved, ultimately seeing that what needed to be published was released to the masses, while transporting many letters, private papers, manuscripts, and notebooks to the Bodleian Library at Oxford.

It is an understatement to say that Hooper was greatly impacted by Jack. I heard him say with my own ears that "Jack was the most Christian man I had ever met."[37] Quite a statement for anyone to make. It seems to go beyond merely admiring a person, to what one might call hero worship, which is actually how Hooper described it: "I hero-worshipped him, and still do. I can't think of a better way of spending my life than by making his contribution better known."[38] These are powerful words from a humble and soft-spoken servant, who has loudly and profoundly preserved the voice of his hero.

His Nemesis: Elizabeth Anscombe

It wasn't really that big of a thing in her mind. She didn't necessarily disagree with him totally either, it was just the way in which he had worded it.[39]

PAUL SHAKESHAFT

While *nemesis* may be too harsh a term when speaking of Elizabeth Anscombe (1919–2001) in relation to C. S. Lewis, she is most certainly remembered as the one who confronted him and took him to task publicly, and depending upon whose version of the

36. Sharp, "Rescued from the Bonfire."

37. Walter Hooper, in a conversation with the author on June 19, 2018.

38. Lambert, "C. S. Lewis' Other American."

39. Paul Shakeshaft, interview by author on May 10, 2019. Shakeshaft was one of the resident scholars who lived at The Kilns. He was also a tour director and student at Oxford. Shakeshaft's supervisor was Roger Scruton, PhD, from Cambridge, where Elizabeth Anscombe was his tutor. The facts shared here were told by Anscombe to Scruton, who then shared them with Shakeshaft.

events one believes, the situation may or may not have had a profound and/or depressing effect on Lewis. Anscombe, a brilliant, brash philosopher, taught at Cambridge University. She was adept in almost every area of philosophy, but is probably best known for the fact that she translated some of her mentor, Ludwig Wittgenstein's most important works, which dealt with linguistics and the nature of language. It is said that she was one of Wittgenstein's favorite students, verified by the fact that he named her as one of three executors of his estate. She possessed an affinity for Cuban cigars, whiskey, and spirited debate. Reputedly fearless (which is probably why she had the courage to confront Lewis), she was an ardent, pro-life Catholic, who on one occasion even chained herself to the doors of an abortion clinic.

The legendary confrontation with Lewis occurred at the Socratic Club dinner on February 2, 1948. While I am not going to delve into the minutiae of their argument, suffice it to say that Anscombe took issue with the way that Lewis had worded his argument in the book *Miracles*, particularly having to do with "Naturalism" and his statement in chapter 3 that it wasn't "valid." While she did not disagree totally with his position, she challenged him to refine and/or rephrase some of his verbiage, especially the term "valid."[40]

Some have claimed that the interaction caused Lewis to become depressed, give up writing apologetics entirely, and turn predominantly to fiction. This claim is simply not true, as Lewis published no fewer than thirty-four apologetic essays after the debate[41] and rewrote chapter 3 of *Miracles*, summarily re-releasing it in 1960. Anscombe wrote a response to the re-release of *Miracles* in *Metaphysics and the Philosophy of Mind: The Collected Papers of G.E.M. Anscombe*, vol. 2, stating that she still didn't totally agree with Lewis, but respected him as a scholar for rewriting and re-releasing his book.[42]

---

40. Gregory Bassham offers a detailed account of the debate in his paper entitled "The Anscombe 'Legend' Is Mostly True."

41. Jerry Root refutes the claim that Lewis was so devastated by the Anscombe debate that he gave up apologetics entirely. See Root, "Dispelling Myths."

42. Anscombe, *Metaphysics and the Philosophy of Mind*, 231.

Mutual Impact?

Might I have included more individuals in this section? Absolutely. There were in fact more Inklings and other influential people who crossed paths with and were involved in Lewis's legacy; however, unless you are a Lewis nerd or scholar (probably both), chances are that you wouldn't even know who they were. Outside of Tolkien and maybe MacDonald, most of the names mentioned in this section have not been widely read, nor would they be recognized by the general public . . . but for the most part, Lewis is. And, it is he who stimulates you to meet the people in this chapter, maybe even read their works and/or study their lives. It is almost never the other way around. Thus, the thesis of this book is substantiated a bit more. The fact of the matter is that through Lewis, you meet his contemporaries, are challenged by him to engage with them for yourself, thereby becoming more literate, more informed, and certainly wondering about reason #3 in my cumulative case.

Reason #3

Because He Invites the Intellect to Kiss the Imagination

I am a rationalist. For me, reason is the natural organ
for truth; but imagination is the organ of meaning.[1]

C. S. LEWIS

Kissing?

MY REASON #3 IS *because he invites the intellect to kiss the imagination.* I am certain that you are wondering what on earth does kissing have to do with this discussion? Well, I don't know about you, but I would rather be kissed than hit on the head with a baseball bat or a hammer. Wouldn't you? Most of us who were raised in the modern era have been taught either overtly, or subconsciously, through the deification of logic and the unequivocal primacy of empirical things, that we should only trust that which we can see, measure, and/or prove. Rationality is encouraged to beat into submission the unprovable, or at least be primary. Thus, dreams, visions, feelings, and imaginary things are to be regarded as subservient to cold, hard facts and laws. We can mostly thank the Enlightenment (I use that term loosely) for that state of affairs. Thinkers in that era told us that spiritual, imaginative, and

1. Lewis, "Bluspels and Flalansferes" 157.

unprovable things must acquiesce to the empirical and provable. In the words of John Locke,

> Nothing that is contrary to, and inconsistent with, the clear and self-evident dictates of reason, has a right to be urged or assented to as a matter of faith, wherein reason has nothing to do.[2]

Contra Locke, Lewis invites his readers to wholeheartedly engage in the "self-evident dictates of reason" as well as the imaginary matters of faith. For him, the faith-filled and imaginative place imbues reason with meaning. No fan of the cultural snobbery perpetuated by the Enlightenment, he urges his readers to think rationally and imagine heartily. He suggests that the logical and reasonable are to be complemented and kissed by the faith-filled and intangible. Imagination doesn't have to be dominated or extinguished by reason, as Locke seems to suggest.

An imaginative technique used skillfully by Lewis to engage his readers in the dance of reason and imagination is a device that he called a "supposal."[3] It would be an invitation offered to his readers to suppose what something might look, act, or play out like in another world or context. This is exactly what he does in *The Great Divorce*, by not overtly stating his support for purgatory, but by challenging readers to suppose, or imagine, what a bus ride to a place between heaven and hell might in fact look like—a place where people might continue their earthly trajectories into eternity. He also does it again and again throughout *The Chronicles of Narnia* as his readers suppose and ponder about the deep, mysterious, redemptive qualities of the real Savior, Jesus, who actually

---

2. Locke, *Essay Concerning Human Understanding*, 2:425–26.

3. The term *supposal* was coined by Lewis. He explains its meaning in a letter to James E. Higgins regarding questions that Higgins had asked him relating to the use of fiction in children's books. See Higgins, "Letter from C. S. Lewis." The actual quote is as follows: "The Narnian books are not as much allegory as supposal. 'Suppose there were a Narnian world and it, like ours, needed redemption. What kind of incarnation and Passion might Christ be supposed to undergo there?'"

came to earth, by meeting in their imaginations, the great lion Aslan who rules in Narnia.

Lewis repeatedly provides opportunities for his readers to engage in this complementary relationship between reason and imagination. He wants them to see, feel, hear, and smell the thoughts that he is rationally, methodically, and logically describing. One of the most masterfully articulated and eerily prophetic examples of his ability to accomplish this can be seen by examining how *The Abolition of Man* (an apologetic work) and *That Hideous Strength* (a science fiction story) complement one another. They both, ultimately, mutually elucidate the same thesis, only in differing formats.

The Abolition of Man exposes the degrading effects of relativism upon western culture, primarily through the baseless, amoral education of innocent school children. In the end, Lewis asserts emphatically that this path will result in mankind's ultimate demise. *That Hideous Strength* vivifies his conclusions, by imagining the actions of a seditious, amoral group of scientists called N.I.C.E., whose intentions aren't quite so nice at all. They call good, bad and bad, good. And to those entrapped in the spell of N.I.C.E., absolutes are tethered to the mysterious utterings of the evil "Head," who is in charge of all things. However, hope is to be hoped for and joy is certainly possible if the right, good, and often unpopular decisions are made, and the reader is invited to hope that the protagonists, a young married couple, Jane and Mark Studdock, will do so. Reason and imagination certainly dance with one another and ultimately kiss when *The Abolition of Man* and *That Hideous Strength* are considered together.

The Short List

While I will concede that there are other influential writers, Ancient, Modern and Postmodern, who have engaged the masses in rational and imaginative thought, the list of those who can actually do or have done this as effectively as Lewis is very, very short. I submit to you that Lewis would be at the head of the list. If you don't believe me, answer this question, "Who would be on your short list?" See what I mean? It is a short list, isn't it? You may not have been able to even come up with one writer at all. Let's give it a go. From the Ancients, maybe it would be Plato and his *Dialogues*, interactions where he urges you to reason at a high level, while at the same time imagining yourself walking with Socrates and him through the cave.

Headlining most modern lists would probably be G. K. Chesterton. If he isn't on the list, he certainly should be. There wasn't anyone more adept at articulating the truths of the faith in palatable fashion. He did so in *The Everlasting Man* and *Orthodoxy* to name only two of his legendary apologetic works. Classic biographical works on the lives of St. Francis of Assisi and St. Thomas Aquinas also flowed from his pen. His *Father Brown Mysteries* certainly engage the imagination as the brilliant fictitious protagonist priest, Father Brown, solves crime after crime, while making powerful moral and spiritual points. Chesterton was masterful at engaging the intellect and the imagination simultaneously. However, I must be truthful with you and confess that I would probably never have even read him had *The Everlasting Man* not been on Lewis's list of "Top Ten Favorite Books" (to be discussed in chapter 5). And that is one of the main emphases of this book; there just seem to be very, very few who were able to do what Lewis did. However, in the name of fairness, let's try and come up with some more names.

How about someone like Aleksandr Solzhenitsyn? Would he be on your list? This mouthpiece for oppressed people used his literary genius to expose the horrors of communism by inviting his readers to enter the struggle to stay alive with protagonist Ivan in the *Gulag Archipelago*. His prolific pen exposed many evils, and he challenged entire nations and won a Nobel Prize in literature. But how many people even know who he is, much less read his books? To prove this point recently, I asked some college students if they had read Solzhenitsyn. They literally had no idea who he was. On a more encouraging note, however, they did know Plato, but all of them confessed that they hadn't read any of his works.

Some of them had thought of it, however, solely because Lewis had challenged them to read old books.

> He would rather read some dreary modern book, ten times as long, all about "isms" and influences and only once in twelve pages telling him what Plato actually said. The error is rather an amiable one, for it springs from humility. The student is half afraid to meet one of the great philosophers face to face. . . . It is a good rule, after reading a new Book, never to allow yourself another new one till you have read an old one in between. If that is too much for you, you should at least read one old one to every three new ones.[4]

A case might be made for a few other influential modern writers. Names such as Sartre and Nietzsche might be considered. They have undoubtedly impacted many with their ability to provoke readers to think, imagine, and feel; but how many of the masses really know who they are, much less read any of their work? Perhaps you have thought of some other names, but I ask you, "Do these authors come close to the sustained, real-life impact that Lewis had and is still having?" Perhaps the great and unassuming Walter Hooper has said it best, "Lewis has probably accomplished as much as any modern writer, both in his fiction and in his sermons, to make heaven believable."[5] And many thanks to our supremely intelligent and imaginative God that he has done so. But, not only has Lewis made the reality of hope for heaven more believable, he has also made living on earth so much more vibrant and imaginatively enjoyable as well. Let's take a look at some of his most heavenly examples by considering reason #4 in my cumulative case.

4. Lewis, "Introduction," 9–10.
5. Hooper, "Introduction."

Reason #4

Because He Knew Aslan

A lion evokes nobility . . . it was only natural that
he made the one who rules Narnia the King of the
beasts . . . a lion. You can't have a platypus do that.[1]

WALTER HOOPER

Why The Lion?

I MUST ADMIT THAT over the course of my life I have felt the ominous, beautiful, present, absent, ornery, glorious, scary, mystical, predictable, unpredictable nature and personality of Jesus, and to be quite honest, I sometimes find myself at a loss for words to describe him. But Lewis has certainly helped me and countless numbers of others, especially in the way that he has brought the real Savior to life through an imaginary lion named Aslan. So, cumulative case reason #4 for "Why Lewis?" is *because he knew Aslan.* In this legendary character, the imaginary has most certainly given meaning to the real. But, have you ever wondered why Lewis chose the lion? I have, and in my opinion there are at least three possibilities and probably more.

1. Hooper, "Life and Writing of C. S. Lewis: Part Three."

Why Lewis?

First, as we have already mentioned, Lewis loved Charles Williams dearly. In 1931 he had written a book that Lewis found "a very great one" entitled *The Place of the Lion*. Could it be that the usage of a lion as the central figure in *The Lion, the Witch and the Wardrobe*, written in 1949 was in homage to his dear friend who had died in 1945? Although I haven't found anything in print to corroborate my hunch, it certainly sounds like the kind of thing Lewis, who loved a good allusion, would have done in remembrance of his gone-but-not-forgotten friend.

Second, Dr. Marvin Hinten, in his book *The Keys to the Chronicles: Unlocking the Symbols of C. S. Lewis's Narnia*[2] postulates that in the late 1940s, Lewis had had a Middle Eastern student, M. A. Manzalaoui, who did his Oxford thesis on various English translations of Arabic works. Lewis, the conscientious tutor, immersed himself in the subject and reread Edward Lane's classic translation of *Arabian Nights*. That being the case, *aslan*, the Turkish word for "lion" was most probably on his mind as he was beginning to write *The Lion, the Witch and the Wardrobe*.

Third, most people understand what Hooper was talking about in the quotation given above, "it is only natural" that a lion rule Narnia. They understand that a lion is powerful, majestic, and strong, basing their opinions solely upon the fact that they have seen one in the zoo or on a screen. However, the inherent knowledge that a lion is king of the beasts was indelibly etched into my mind one dark morning in South Africa. The occasion was during a trip where we had been staying in a bungalow situated on the outskirts of a game park. I was admittedly a bit on edge, due to the fact that there were signs in our hut instructing us to close the rhino gate at night (for obvious reasons) as well as place a long bean bag, situated at the end of our beds in front of the crack under our doors. It was supposed to keep black mambas and cobras from trying to slip in under the threshold and bunk with us. Needless to say, I slept with one eye open and my blankets tucked tightly around my entire body like a mummy.

2. Hinten, *Keys to the Chronicles*, 14.

After several hours of mummified sleeplessness, it was time to carefully, nimbly rise, so as not to awaken any mambas or cobras who may have gotten past the bean bag blockade. Then, in the eerie, misty, pre-dawn darkness, we watchfully opened the rhino gate, and quickly loaded into the jungle-creeper of a jeep that had come to fetch us back to the main lodge. Our open air jeep ride from out in the bush was bumpy, winding, and dusty. Upon reaching the main lodge, we were told by our driver to hop out and wait for our host, who happened to be late.

While nervously waiting in the moonlit lot, a life-altering, fear-inciting, exhilarating thing occurred. A sound pierced the darkness, and it was a sound that defies description, but I will try anyway. It was the synthesis of a growl, a scream, a howl, a freight train, and an explosion. I had never heard anything like it. "What the H#!L was that?" said one of our shocked team members as we heard it. Then, at the same time, in unison we screamed, "A LION!!! OH MY GOD . . . A LION!" There was no doubt as to what we had just heard, and equally as little doubt that there was an ominous creature in close proximity.

Once we were thankfully and safely situated in the vehicle that seemed to take forever to reach us, we recounted the roar to our host. "That was the king, letting everyone know that he was awake," he said calmly. The roar was beautiful, terrible, awe-inspiring, and fear-inducing, all at the same time. After that experience, I have no doubt why it would be natural for Lewis to choose a beast who could make that type of sound to be the king of his Narnian world. The unmistakable roar certainly gave me a new context as I thought about the eternal, victorious roar of The Lion of the Tribe of Judah. Yes, he is awake . . . he has risen from his sleep . . . and he has risen indeed!

Aslan Gives Me Words

While the unmistakable roar of the real lion I described in the previous section undoubtedly helped me to imagine the powerful living presence of the real King Jesus, words from or about the imaginary lion Aslan, have helped me to describe the actual Lion of Heaven, on countless occasions. And while each person reading this book probably has his or her own favorites, my top four Aslan quotes or descriptions are as follows.

Without a doubt, *number one* for me has to be "Aslan is on the move." The first time that I read it was a eureka moment for me. Here is the place in *The Lion, the Witch and the Wardrobe* where Mr. Beaver utters this most memorable phrase:

> "They say Aslan is on the move—perhaps has already landed." And now a very curious thing happened. None of the children knew who Aslan was, any more than you do; but the moment the Beaver had spoken these words everyone felt quite different . . . at the name of Aslan each one of the children felt something jump on the inside of it.[3]

Something jumped on the inside of me when I heard it for the first time too. Lewis, through the mouth of Mr. Beaver had articulated what I had felt about Jesus for many years, but didn't know exactly how to say. The fact that He was, is, and always has been directly involved in my life was apparent. And while I may not have been able to pinpoint it, I had known it down in "my knower." It now made sense. I now had some imaginative language to express what I felt about what I knew. He was certainly "on the move."

My family and friends have used this helpful "beaver-speak" innumerable times over the years. One of us just has to say to the other, "He's on the move," and immediately we know that Jesus is doing something to which we should pay close attention. Yes, along with Mr. Beaver and all true Narnians, we too are aware that the Lion, Jesus, has most certainly landed and is on the move in more ways than we can count.

Number two on my list is yet another quote from the inimitable Mr. Beaver as he describes Aslan to Susan and Lucy, who had not yet met the One who ruled Narnia:

> "Ooh!" said Susan, "I'd thought he was a man. Is he—quite safe? I shall feel rather nervous about meeting a lion."

---

3. Lewis, *Lion, the Witch and the Wardrobe*, 74.

"That you will, dearie, and make no mistake," said Mrs. Beaver; "if there's anyone who can appear before Aslan without their knees knocking, they're either braver than most or else just silly."

"Then he isn't safe?" said Lucy.

"Safe?" said Mr. Beaver; "don't you hear what Mrs. Beaver tells you? Who said anything about safe? 'Course he isn't safe. But he's good. He's the King I tell you."[4]

My original intent as I wrote this section of the book was to search for and include specific Scripture references that would elucidate this. What does it mean to be both good and safe? In my mind, someone who is "safe" in this context is someone who lives a non-threatening, uneventful, no-risk, status-quo life. One who wouldn't rock the boat or ruffle any feathers. There are plenty of biblical references that speak of the goodness or omni-benevolence of Jesus. There are also plenty of references that speak of his awesome power or omnipotence. However, there are equally as many verses that prove that he was anything but "safe" in the status-quo sense of being safe. He pushed over tables in the temple, whipped people, and dared religious zealots to try and go through him to get to a woman they had caught in adultery.

I must admit that I was hard-pressed to find texts that spoke of all of these aspects of his nature in one statement. Good . . . powerful . . . safe. Therein lies the beauty and the power of the fictional picture. Through appealing to our imaginations, Lewis helps us to see what is true and real. His picture vivifies what Scripture verifies. Aslan and Jesus are both "good, but not safe."

In Aslan, we see the all-powerful king of the beasts, ruling, roaring, and restoring order to Narnia. One who is fiercely powerful, but always good. What an amazing picture of Jesus these images paint for us. He was and is the Omnipotent One, yet lived in close proximity to his friends. So close, that on one occasion after sliding to the back of the boat to take a nap, he was hastily awakened by them for fear of drowning in a squall. Upset and put

4. Lewis, *Lion, the Witch and the Wardrobe*, 86.

off, he summarily scolded the wind and waves in holy anger as he screamed, "Quiet! Be still!" (Mark 4:39).[5]

Then, undoubtedly with water dripping from his furrowed brow, he wondered out loud to his disciples, "Why are you so afraid? Do you still have no faith?" (Mark 4:40). As he laid back down to finish his nap, I am sure that they stood drenched and trembling in the wake of his awesome power. Trembling, not in fear that he would harm them, for he was good, but trembling because he was crazy powerful. Good he was, yes, but he was certainly not someone who was content with a status quo that meant sinking with a posse of faithless men in a storm. They had to be asking themselves, "Who was this man who possessed so much authority that he could scold nature's elements as if they were domesticated animals?" Yet, he napped with them, laughed with them, ate with them, and sat little children on his lap? The Lion of the Tribe of Judah he was. A good and wild lion who was certainly not safe.

Number three on my list grows out of and is essentially an addendum to *number two*. It has to do with Aslan inviting the girls, Susan and Lucy, to get close to him:

> "Are you ill dear Aslan?" asked Susan.
>
> "No," said Aslan. "I am sad and lonely. Lay your hands on my mane, so that I can feel you are there and let us walk like that."
>
> And so the girls did what they would never have dared to do without his permission, but what they had longed to do ever since they first saw him—buried their cold hands in the beautiful sea of fur and stroked it and, so doing, walked with him.[6]

What a beautiful depiction of the cry of our hearts toward Jesus. Because he is so good, we want desperately to be with him; but because he is the One who loudly roars with all of the power of the Godhead, we must never be too presumptuous. Like Aslan, Jesus invites us to come close—to walk with him, to lean on him, and

---

5. All biblical quotations are from the New International Version (NIV), unless otherwise indicated.

6. Lewis, *Lion, the Witch and the Wardrobe*, 156.

to even touch him. In the same way that the girls stroked Aslan's mane, we too can get close and touch God through reaching out to Jesus. He invites us all to do this. He gives us permission. The Gospels are replete with example after example.

> Then he said to Thomas, "Put your finger here; see my hands. Reach out your hand and put it into my side. Stop doubting and believe." (John 20:27)

> One of them, the disciple whom Jesus loved was reclining next to Him. . . . Leaning back against Jesus (John 13:23, 25)

> Just then a woman who had been subject to bleeding for twelve years came up behind him and touched the edge of his cloak. (Matt 9:20)

> Those troubled by impure spirits were cured, and the people all tried to touch him, because power was coming from him and healing them all. (Luke 6:18–19)

> A man with leprosy came and knelt before him and said, "Lord, if you are willing, you can make me clean." Jesus reached out his hand and touched the man. (Matt 8:2–3)

> People were bringing little children to Jesus for him to place his hands on them, but the disciples rebuked them. When Jesus saw this, he was indignant. He said to them, "Let the little children come to me, and do not hinder them, for the kingdom of God belongs to such as these. Truly I tell you, anyone who will not receive the kingdom of God like a little child will never enter it." And he took the children in his arms, placed his hands on them and blessed them. (Mark 10:14–16)

Whether by the lion in Narnia or the Resurrected Lion of Judah, we are invited, along with the inquisitive girls, lepers, the sick, the young, and the skeptical Apostle to touch him and together walk closely. And when we do, we are saved, healed, filled, calmed, resurrected, and set free.

Number four for me is undoubtedly one of the best descriptions of heaven that I have ever heard. I have used it time and time again to describe the actual place where we will live in our eternal glory. The following words aren't directly from the mouth of Aslan, but from the unicorn in *The Last Battle* where he describes Aslan's domain, the true Narnia:

> It was the Unicorn who summed up what everyone was feeling. He stamped his right fore-hoof on the ground and neighed and then cried: "I have come home at last! This is my real country! I belong here. This is the land I have been looking for all my life, though I never knew it until now. The reason why we loved the old Narnia is that sometimes it looked a little bit like this. Bree-hee-hee! Come further up, come further in!"[7]

He speaks of that "further up and further in" place to which Aslan refers throughout the entirety of *The Chronicles*. A place so big and so vibrant that it cannot really be adequately described. So huge that it cannot be fully explored. So dreamlike and vivid that it couldn't be real; but in reality it was, is, and forever will be. A place where one could actually fly without plunging to his death. A place where one could run without becoming weary. A place of reunions to be had with lost loved ones; and together, with The Lion, in their youthful glory, everyone parties, sings, and imbibes in the real elixir that is true life. This place is an indescribably unreal reality. It is a dream come true times infinity.

The images of Aslan's domain being described as the place that can only be plumbed by going "further up and further in" hearkens to the words of Jesus speaking of his domain:

> Do not let your hearts be troubled. You believe in God; believe also in me. My Father's house has many rooms; if that were not so, would I have told you that I am going there to prepare a place for you? And if I go and prepare a place for you, I will come back and take you to be with me that you also may be where I am. You know the way to the place where I am going. (John 14:1–4)

7. Lewis, *Last Battle*, 171.

The Apostle John describes Jesus's "further up and further in" place like this:

> "Look! God's dwelling place is now among the people, and he will dwell with them. They will be his people, and God himself will be with them and be their God. 'He will wipe every tear from their eyes. There will be no more death' or mourning or crying or pain, for the old order of things has passed away." He who was seated on the throne said, "I am making everything new!" (Rev 21:3–5)

Everything new? How much is everything, and how new is new? This sounds just too good to be true, doesn't it? After mentioning this type of eternity in a sermon, I was approached by one of our leaders afterwards. With a quizzical look on his face he said, "Pastor, if God is omnipotent and heaven is as big as you say, is it possible for him to create something so big that even he can't explore all of it?" I hadn't been asked that before, so I stood and pondered for a bit. Then these words came to my mind. "I don't know if I can answer that exactly, but I do know this, in heaven we are always moving further up and further in. The past and the future are swallowed up in the now and the new. Things are continuously being made new through and with Jesus. He is the focus of the old and the hope of a new that never ends. He is the further up and further in One." We both just stood there and considered what I had said. Lewis's fictional description of the actuality of the further up and further in place in Jesus helped us make sense of the extrasensory, mind-boggling eternity that is heaven with him.

This is the Hope of Glory for which we were created and truly yearn. We were created to live in the reality of further up and further in, but unless we can imagine it, feel it, and maybe even smell it, we can never really see it. Thank God for the Lion who has helped me imagine these things. For he is good but not safe, always on the move, and ever leading us further up and further in.

> And as He spoke He no longer looked to them like a lion, but the things that began to happen after that were so great and beautiful that I cannot write them. And for us, this is the end of all the stories, and we can most truly say

that they all lived happily ever after. But for them, it was only the beginning of the real story. All their life in this world and all their adventures in Narnia had only been the cover and the title page: now at last they were beginning Chapter One of the Great Story, which no one on earth has read: which goes on forever and ever: in which every chapter is better than the one before.[8]

Let's start reading that book and living that story this very minute. Bree-hee-hee. And with imaginations thoroughly stimulated and piqued, it is time to engage the intellect to as a high a level as possible and transition to reason #5 in my cumulative case.

8. Lewis, *Last Battle*, 183–84.

Reason #5

Because He Issues the Challenge to Read Old Books

The only safety is to have a standard of plain, central
Christianity ("mere Christianity" as Baxter called
it) which puts the controversies of the moment
in their proper perspective. Such a standard
can be acquired only from the old books.

C. S. LEWIS[1]

BOOKS, BOOKS, AND MORE books. It is said that at one time Lewis had over five thousand of them in his home. Stacks were everywhere. Standing at attention in his bedroom, the sitting room, the music room, and his rooms at both Oxford and Cambridge, always ready to assault ignorance at first sight. Books filled both his days and nights as a little boy, remaining a constant companion, until the end of his days as an old man. "You can never get a cup of tea large enough, or a book long enough, to suit me,"[2] was a maxim that he spent countless hours applying. The longest of books and cup after cup of tea were his rule.

1. Lewis, "Introduction," 10.
2. Lewis, while this quote is popularly ascribed to Lewis the exact literary address could not be established.

Since he was such a vocal proponent of engaging with all sorts of books, in 1962 the editors of *The Christian Century* magazine thought it might be interesting to ask him the following question, "What books did most to shape your vocational attitude and your philosophy of life?"[3] In what I will refer to as "The List" Lewis elucidates his love for both old and new books of varying genres. Quite a broad spectrum of subjects and authors are present, and you will note that he stuck closely to his rule of one old book for every new one, with a pattern of five modern followed by five pre-modern.

Admittedly, some of these authors and their works might not be your cup of tea, but because they had such an impact on Lewis's life, work, and development, undoubtedly you will be compelled to engage with them. And this fact alone brings us once again to our thesis, that there is just no one quite like Lewis. Because he was and is so influential, we want to forgo our own tastes and get a taste of what made him tick. So, reason #5 is the challenge that he issues to read old books. Classics are on The List and some that you have never heard of . . . yet. But, I'm guessing that the force that is Lewis will push and prod you to stretch yourself, meet these authors, and engage with them personally. Even if you don't care for them like Lewis did, you will think in broader, deeper, and more Lewisian fashion because of the experience.

The List

Since the purpose of this section is to introduce you to Lewis's list, I will not give my impression of the books contained on it. In a select few instances, I will give my opinions as to the impact of a particular book upon Lewis, but for the most part I will not delve too deeply into those types of conjecture.[4] Thus, I will first intro-

---

3. "Books That Have Influenced," 575–76. Note that respondents could provide up to ten titles, other than the Bible. Results were published in *The Christian Century*, see Lewis, "Ex Libris," 719.

4. In their book, *C. S. Lewis's List: The Ten Books That Influenced Him Most*, editors David Werther and Susan Werther have delved deeply into each of the books on The List and why Lewis might have felt so strongly about them.

duce each book or author with pertinent Lewis quotes; second, I will give a brief overview of the book, then, the rest is up to you. Consider the gauntlet thrown. Will you pick it up? I challenge you to do so! Pick up an old book, pour a cup of coffee, or if you want to go totally Lewis, make it a really large cup of tea, then read, re-read, or re-re-read all of the books on The List.

1. *Phantastes* by George MacDonald[5]

It must be more than thirty-years ago that I bought—
almost unwillingly, for I had looked at that volume
on the bookstall and rejected it on a dozen previous
occasions—the Everyman edition of *Phantastes*. A few
hours later I knew that I had crossed a great frontier. . . .
What it actually did to me was to convert, even to baptize
my imagination. . . . The pill was gold all through. . . . The
quality which had enchanted me in his imaginative works
turned out to be the quality of the real universe, the divine,
magical, terrifying and ecstatic reality in which we all live.[6]

C. S. LEWIS

The first book on The List, *Phantastes*, was published in 1858. In it, the author George MacDonald pays homage to Romantic authors William Blake and Percy Shelley with the subtitle "A Faerie Romance for Men and Women." The prevalent themes in *Phantastes* are morality, chivalry, courage, and seeing beyond the surface of things, all within the context of a spiritual pilgrimage. The protagonist Anodos (which means *pathless* in Greek) learns life-changing lessons in a fantasy world, then seeks to apply them in the real, everyday world.

The story begins as Anodos awakens in a dazed and confused state, trying to recall what had happened the night before on his

5. MacDonald, *Phantastes*.
6. Lewis, "Preface," xxxvii.

twenty-first birthday. He recalls that somehow he had inherited several mysterious items from his father, the first item being a sprite, who identifies herself as his "fairy-grandmother." She instructs him to go to Fairy Land. Thinking this absurd, he goes back to sleep. While sleeping . . . or awake (the reader will have to decide), Anodos ends up in a forest, on a journey, where he meets various entities with whom he has conversations about truth and beauty.

One of the entities that he meets, and ultimately pursues while on his journey, is a marble statue of a beautiful woman. In pursuit of her, he engages with talking trees, inhabitants of cottages, and other entities that vie for his love and attention. Ultimately, Anodos, in the midst of his pursuit, is rescued from imminent peril, by Sir Percival, a gallant knight. However, during this time, a "shadow" begins to follow Anodos, incessantly questioning and mocking him in his quest. Percival teaches Anodos about bravery and the pursuit of a noble and good life, while the shadow tries to convince him that his efforts to live well and vibrant are futile.

Anodos's journey becomes a quest, then ultimately a life and death struggle, in which he finds himself fighting a gory battle with good and evil at every turn. In the crucible that ensues, he discovers that sometimes good and evil don't look so obvious. As to how the journey ends and who is victorious in this epic struggle, you will have to walk with Anodos, his shadow, and Sir Percival yourself.

2. *The Everlasting Man* by G. K. Chesterton[7]

Have you tried Chesterton's *The Everlasting
Man*? The best popular apologetic I know.[8]

C. S. LEWIS

---

7. Chesterton, *Everlasting Man*.
8. Vanauken, *Severe Mercy*, 89–90.

Reason #5: Because He Issues the Challenge to Read Old Books

> For a good ("popular") defense of our position against
> modern waffle, to fall back on, I know nothing better
> than G. K. Chesterton's *The Everlasting Man.*[9]

C. S. LEWIS

Although Lewis and Chesterton never met officially, unofficially they engaged with one another at least thirty times via the written word.[10] Of the thirty interactions, the most impactful seems to have been, hands down, the second book on The List, entitled *The Everlasting Man*. In it, Lewis found for the first time, a reasonable defense for the history of the world. Written as a response to H. G. Wells's *The Outline of History*, it was a Christocentric, rational explanation for the existence, trajectory, and ultimate hope for mankind. The book's central theme asserts that when Christ steps onto the stage of history, the entire story begins to take shape and have context. Christ is, in fact, the extraordinary context that fulfills the yearning of mankind throughout history; no ordinary man was he.

Chesterton takes aim at evolutionary theory on several fronts. First, there is man's ability to reason. For him, human intelligence is unsurpassed in accomplishment and potentiality. Second, he asserts that one has to look only as far as early cave-art to see that man has been drawing and painting since time immemorial. Apes simply have not, cannot, nor will they ever be able to climb to the artistic heights and abilities of homo sapiens. Third, the religions, philosophies, and accompanying mythologies that have developed over the eons are undoubtedly best, and most fully satisfied in the true, Christian myth. Fourth, laughter is to be seen as something that distinguishes man from the beasts. It is a trait inherently placed in them as an *imago* of their Creator, who invariably laughs himself. These are only a few of the bricks laid in the foundation of his case against evolution, but ultimately, Chesterton posits that

9. Lewis, *Collected Letters*, vol. 2, 823.

10. Chesterton scholar Dale Ahlquist states that Lewis owned at least thirty books written by Chesterton, in which he had marked in the margins. Dale Ahlquist, "G. K. Chesterton & C. S. Lewis."

the more man is examined and compared to the animals, the less he actually looks like one.

3. *The Aeneid* by Virgil[11]

All through the poem we are turning that corner. It is this which gives the reader of the *Aeneid* the sense of having lived through so much. No man who has once read it with full perception remains an adolescent."[12]

C. S. LEWIS

The third book on The List was written by Roman poet, Publius Vergilius Maro (70–19 BCE), or Virgil as he has come to be more widely known. He wrote his epic poem *The Aeneid* between the years 30 BCE and 19 BCE. Known as the national poet of Rome, he was quite prolific. In addition to *The Aeneid*, he wrote such classic works as *Eclogues* and *Georgics*, but *The Aeneid* remains his most lasting and broadly impactful work. Before his death, he had set out on a journey to Greece (the setting of *The Aeneid*) where he had anticipated a three-year, pre-publishing time of refining and completing his magnum opus. Unfortunately, en route to Greece he would become gravely ill, finding it necessary to return to Italy, ultimately dying in the historic city of Brundisium. Although his dying wish was for the epic poem to be burned upon his passing, thankfully Caesar Augustus countermanded Virgil's desires, and the poem stands as an enduring literary monument to ancient Greco-Roman civilization.

In *The Aeneid*'s twelve books, Virgil tells the epic story of Rome's founder, Aeneas, son of Prince Anchises and the goddess Aphrodite, ancestors of the twins Romulus and Remus. Through Aeneas's journeys, Virgil proclaims the Roman mission to civilize the world under divine guidance. The reader is introduced to such

11. Virgil, *Aeneid*.

12. Lewis, *Preface to Paradise Lost*, 33–34.

legendary literary characters as Dido, Queen of Carthage; the warrior Turnus, son of Daunus, and the nymph Venilia; the ghost of Aeneas's father, Anchises; and ultimately the eagle-god Jupiter as he utters prophecies regarding Rome's ultimate destiny to conquer the world in war and then to spread civilization and the rule of law among all peoples.

4. *The Temple* by George Herbert[13]

But the most alarming of all was George Herbert. Here was
a man who seemed to me to excel all the authors I had ever
read in conveying the very quality of life as we actually live
it from moment to moment; but the wretched fellow, instead
of doing it all directly, insisted on mediating it through
what I would still have called "the Christian mythology."[14]

C. S. LEWIS

Do you read George Herbert—If what soul doth feel
sometimes my soul might always feel—(George, Herbert,
The Temple (1633), "The Tempter," I, 3–4) He's a good
poet and one who helped to bring me back to the Faith.[15]

C. S. LEWIS

Due to the fact that Lewis was a world class literary scholar (see his tome *Poetry and Prose in the Sixteenth Century*), it isn't surprising that the third book on The List, is George Herbert's (1593–1633) spiritual classic entitled *The Temple*. Throughout the entirety of the 1600s, Herbert was influential, both in life and death. In the seventeenth century alone, there were at least eleven editions of *The Temple*, the first being published posthumously in 1633. As a poet,

13. Herbert, *Temple*.
14. Lewis, *Surprised by Joy*, 237.
15. Lewis, *Collected Letters*, vol. 3, 105–6.

his work falls between the ages of Shakespeare and Milton, and he would probably be more popularly regarded had it not been for those two literary giants. For Lewis, however, in his own personal spiritual formation, it was not necessarily Herbert's ability as a writer, scholar, or statesman that was primary; it was his brilliant and cohesive synthesis of these aspects of his calling within the context of a powerful and vibrant Christian faith that Lewis referred to earlier as the historical and living "Christian mythology."

In *The Temple*, Herbert presents 162 of his poems in an architectural context, using the church building or "temple" as a metaphor for the life of the follower of Christ. It is filled with explicitly biblical poems that meditate on specific verses or thoughts taken directly from Scripture. The first section entitled "The Church-porch" invites the reader to come up and into the place where true, satisfying, and beautiful community with the Creator occurs. The second section, which includes the majority of the poems, is entitled "The Church," and it encompasses any and every subject, theme, holiday, and issue pertinent to the healthy and holy life of the follower of Jesus. Poems dealing with the altar, sacrifice, thanksgiving, redemption, sin, Good Friday, Easter, baptism, Scripture, and true Christian love are included and make up only a few of the offerings. The final section is entitled "The Church militant" and comprises a lengthy poem that gives an overview of church history from Genesis through Christ's ultimate and victorious return.

5. *The Prelude* by William Wordsworth[16]

The Prelude has accompanied me through all
the stages of my pilgrimage: it and the *Aeneid*
(which I never feel you value sufficiently) are the
two long poems to which I most often return.[17]

C. S. LEWIS

16. Wordsworth, *Prelude*.
17. Lewis, *Collected Letters*, vol. 3, 111.

Lewis often alluded to or directly quoted from the fifth book on The List, *The Prelude*. In the above quote, he affirms its importance in his own personal spiritual formation. The inclusion of it in The List can't be overlooked due to the fact other epic poems, such as Milton's *Paradise Lost*, did not even make the cut. His own book, *A Preface to Paradise Lost*, is still highly regarded in the world of literary criticism, and it was common knowledge that he esteemed the epic poem greatly. So, why *The Prelude* and not *Paradise Lost*, *The Iliad*, *The Odyssey*, or another epic poem?

In my opinion, the reason for this was primarily Wordsworth's persistent, mysterious, and mythical description of "joy," a term that he would reference no less than forty-five times in *The Prelude*. This persistence would awaken Lewis to a revelation that joy was more than a mere feeling. It was a sensation that could come suddenly, often unannounced, drawing him somewhere beyond this life. It actually incited in him a desire to question whether or not he might have been created to yearn for the source of joy . . . the joy-giver.

What he read in the opening lines of Wordsworth's legendary poem "Surprised by Joy" undoubtedly touched Lewis deep in his soul. So much so that it would play a central role, not only in his own conversion, but in his approach to apologetics. Thus, as a tip of his hat to Wordsworth and his *Prelude*, Lewis would entitle his own autobiography, *Surprised by Joy*, even quoting from Wordsworth on the title page. Themes of nature, reason, imagination, and perhaps above all, joy, are what scholar Mary Ritter believes were the most profound influences on Lewis. She considers Lewis's *Surprised by Joy* a retelling of *The Prelude* and his own allegorical conversion story, *Pilgrim's Regress*, directly modeled after it stylistically.[18]

Begun in 1798, Wordsworth worked on *The Prelude* his entire life. It was published posthumously, three months after his death in 1850. Originally entitled *Poem to Coleridge: Growth of a Poet's Mind*, it ultimately consisted of thirteen books of blank verse (meaning that it was not lyrical, but conversational). Each of

18. Ritter, "William Wordsworth," 93–94.

the books are entitled corresponding to a period in Wordsworth's life. Titles such as "Introduction—Childhood and School-Time," "School-Time (cont.)," "Residence at Cambridge," and "Summer Vacation," are the titles of the first four books respectively. In many of the books he speaks of his sister Dorothy and his dear friend, poet Samuel Taylor Coleridge. Conversations reflecting on the nature of humanity and recurrent praise of the Divine and overarching order of nature are present throughout.

6. *The Idea of the Holy* by Rudolf Otto[19]

In all developed religion we find three strands or elements,
and in Christianity one more. The first of these is what
Professor Otto calls the experience of the Numinous.[20]

C. S. LEWIS

Rudolf Otto (1869–1937) was a German theologian, philosopher, and historian of religion. Otto is known worldwide for his work regarding man's experience of "the holy," though *The Idea of the Holy* (1923), the sixth book on The List, was his most important book. Otto became well known for participating in Christian ecumenical activities, especially as they related to concerns between Christianity and other religions of the world. This was due in great part to his conviction that there were major commonalities in "all" developed religions.

In *The Idea of the Holy*, these major commonalities, in Otto's opinion, were connected to what he termed the *numinous*. In coining this term, he used a combination of the Latin, *numen* (deity or religious power) and *omen* (a momentous sign). The numinous was to be seen as an awe-inspiring element of religious experience. Otto contended that all of the major developed religions pointed towards this awe-inspiring experience and that Jesus was the

19. Otto, *Idea of the Holy*.
20. Lewis, *Problem of Pain*, 3.

ultimate personification of it. Therefore, he believed that Christians should use this understanding to engage with adherents of other religions to help them see the whole truth, not merely the partial truth expressed in their own religion. Otto's verbiage in *The Idea of the Holy* coupled with what Tolkien would later present to him as the "True Myth"[21] of Christianity would enlighten Lewis to an understanding of the centrality of Christ as the actual Incarnation of the Numinous—a fact that he believed set Christianity apart from any and every other religion.

7. *The Consolation of Philosophy* by Boethius[22]

For centuries one of the most influential books ever
written in Latin . . . until about two hundred years ago
it would, I think, have been hard to find an educated
man in any European country who did not love it.[23]

C. S. LEWIS

Anicius Manlius Severinus Boethius (c. 477–524 CE) was a Roman philosopher, theologian, and statesman who served as an advisor to the gothic king Theodoric. Sometime around 523 CE, he was convicted of conspiracy and treason, ultimately being sentenced to death and executed in 524 CE. While awaiting execution, he wrote the seventh book on The List, *The Consolation of Philosophy*. In *The Consolation* Boethius endeavors to find the nature of true happiness by entering into a dialogue between his imprisoned self and Philosophy, personified as a woman. Utilizing both prose and lyrical verse, the conversation is organized into five books.

In book one, Boethius tells the story of his grief at being in prison while awaiting execution. Book two is Philosophy's poetic response to Boethius's grief. She exhorts him toward a place of

---

21. The "True Myth" will be the focus of the next chapter.
22. Boethius, *Consolation of Philosophy*.
23. Lewis, *Discarded Image*, 75.

healing, a healing that would undoubtedly come because he was nourished on the milk of Philosophy. Book three records a hope-filled response from Boethius, followed by Philosophy's encouragement to him. This encouragement reminded him of honored men such as Anaxagoras, Socrates, Zeno, and Seneca, who all suffered valiantly against corruption and hypocrisy. Some of them even died nobly for their convictions.

In book four, Boethius laments that evil people are like beasts, free to bring destruction to good people. Philosophy objects, making her point that evil people are not truly free, due to the fact that even when they achieve their desires to do evil, they are the ones who really suffer. In book five, Boethius and Philosophy discuss God's foreknowledge. She challenges him ultimately to have faith in God, the only one who is fully provident . . . even in death.

8. *The Life of Samuel Johnson* by James Boswell[24]

And surely everyone knows who they are: Plato's Socrates,
the Jesus of the Gospels, and Boswell's Johnson. Our
acquaintance with them shows itself in a dozen ways.[25]

C. S. LEWIS

The eighth book on The List is *The Life of Samuel Johnson* by James Boswell (1740–1795). As evidenced in the above quote, Lewis elevated it stylistically to a status akin to the likes of Plato and the Gospel writers. Many have agreed with Lewis's assessment, so much so that *The Life of Samuel Johnson* is considered to be one of the best biographies ever written in the English language.

Boswell acquired fame initially because of his penchant for securing interviews with cultural icons the likes of Rousseau,

24. Boswell, *Life of Samuel Johnson.*

25. Lewis, "Fern-Seed and Elephants." This work was originally entitled "Modern Theology and Biblical Criticism," and Lewis read this essay at West-cott House, Cambridge, on May 11, 1959. It was published under that title in *Christian Reflections* (1981), and it is now in *Fern-seed and Elephants* (1998).

Voltaire, and Corsican chieftain Pasquale de Paoli. As a trial attorney, he was often engaged in cross-examinations and dialogues that invariably honed his skills of observation, especially as they pertained to one-on-one conversations that fostered his ability to see and articulate verbally even the minutest of details. Elected to a prestigious organization known as The Club in 1773, he would meet and befriend Dr. Samuel Johnson. Later in that same year, Johnson and Boswell would make a legendary tour of The Hebrides. It was on this trip that Boswell kept the detailed journals that would become the foundation for the manuscript of *The Life of Samuel Johnson*, which would ultimately be published in two volumes in 1791.

Johnson, the subject of Boswell's biography, was literally born into books, as his mother delivered him in a bed above his father's bookshop in 1709. From that day forward he would be surrounded by, engrossed in, and ultimately known for the written word. At three years old, he showed such exceptional intelligence that his parents frequently asked him to perform amazing stunts of memory. As a child prodigy, Johnson excelled greatly in school, especially in writing. Eventually, he secured work as a journalist and wrote many and varied types of articles for *The Gentlemen's Magazine* between 1741 and 1744.

While the prolific Johnson would continue to engage in varying genres of literature, in 1746, a group of publishers would pitch to him the project for which he would personally become most renowned—the writing of a complete dictionary of the English language. At the expense of his own personal welfare, over the next ten years, he worked tirelessly on the project, finally publishing *A Dictionary of the English Language* in 1755. In 1762, the government granted Johnson, greatly diminished and in deteriorating health by this time, an annual pension in appreciation of his monumental work on the *Dictionary*.

In 1773, Johnson's health took another turn for the worse when he suffered a stroke and lost the ability to speak. Many came to visit Johnson in his declining state over the next decade, including Boswell, who was actually with Johnson when he died on December 13, 1784. While Samuel Johnson was undoubtedly famous in his own time and in his own right, Boswell's recording of their travels and interactions in *The Life of Samuel Johnson* has become much more renowned than its subject.

9. *Descent into Hell* by Charles Williams[26]

Have you read C. William's *Descent into Hell*?
If not, do so at once.[27]

C. S. LEWIS

Lewis's personal relationship with Charles Williams has already been addressed in detail in chapter 2, so there is nothing more to add in regard to who he was historically and the profound impact that he and Lewis had upon one another. However, *Descent into Hell*, the ninth book on The List, written by Williams, was one that Lewis encouraged those close to him to "read at once"; therefore, a closer look at the book about which he was so emphatic is certainly warranted.

Written in 1937, *Descent into Hell* is a psychological thriller with deep spiritual overtones. It chronicles the spiritual journeys of three inhabitants of a quiet fictitious English suburb called Battle Hill. These journeys are set against the backdrop of a play written by Peter Stanhope, the local poet/playwright. The first journey is that of an unnamed suicide victim, trapped in a place in time in which he killed himself, and he seems to be awaiting his eternal fate. The second journey, is that of Pauline Anstruther, a woman haunted by her doppelgänger, which comes a little closer each time it appears. She lives in terror that one day she will meet this apparition and suffer a terrible fate. The third journey is that of a man named Lawrence Wentworth, a celebrated academic who is enamored with the heroine of Stanhope's play, Adela Hunt. When Hunt does not affectionately return his advances,

---

26. Williams, *Descent into Hell*.
27. Lewis, *Collected Letters*, vol. 2, 672.

he finds himself propelled into a sea of self-pity so deep and in-sidious that it gives birth to a demonic succubus of Adela who becomes the focus of his love.

Two main intertwining themes are prevalent in the book. The first and most prominent is that of "the doctrine of substituted love." This doctrine takes Paul's command in Gal 6:2 to "bear one another's burdens" literally. By literally, it is meant that an indi-vidual can take on the actual fears or troubles of another. When Pauline shares her fears with Stanhope, he presents this doctrine to her, offering to take them upon himself. Williams believed that this was, in fact, a law of the universe for all.[28] Lewis was convinced that substitution had actually occurred for his wife, Joy, when after asking for her suffering to be given to him, he became sick and she went miraculously into remission for a period of time.

The second theme that is prevalent in *Descent into Hell* is that of self-love. While several characters wrestle with it to some extent, it is Wentworth's self-love that is the worst and ultimately causes his demise. As a result of not possessing Adela for himself, his own insidious romantic desires become the focus of his life. The book, in fact, closes with Wentworth retreating into his own private uni-verse as he helplessly dotes over his magical demonic-lover.

---

28. Andrew C. Stout covers this subject in depth in his paper entitled "'It Was Allowed to One': C. S. Lewis on the Practice of Substitution."

10. *Theism and Humanism* by Arthur James Balfour[29]

There is a dignity and poignancy in the bare fact that
a thing exists. Thus, as Balfour pointed out in *Theism
and Humanism* (a book too little read), there are
many historical facts which we should not applaud for
any obvious humour or pathos if we supposed them
to be inventions; but once we believe them to be real,
we have, in addition to our intellectual satisfaction,
a certain aesthetic delight in the idea of them.[30]

C. S. LEWIS

Last, but not least, is book number ten on The List, *Theism and Humanism* by Arthur James Balfour (1848–1930). Balfour was a powerful and influential British statesman, who was a contemporary of Winston Churchill, G. K. Chesterton, and Neville Chamberlain. He held various positions of power in government for over fifty years, but is most noted for his World War I statement (the Balfour Declaration), when, as Prime Minister, he expressed the official British approval of Zionism, ultimately paving the way for a Jewish state. While he was obviously influential because of his political acumen, he was also a brilliant philosopher, lecturer, prolific author, and essayist.

Theism and Humanism was originally presented as a series of ten lectures, known as the Gifford Lectures and delivered at the University of Glasgow. Balfour's main intention was to explain "Divine Knowledge" so that the "plain man" might be able to understand the bridge between philosophy and science. He believed that in doing so, he could establish a foundation for a set of values, knowledge of the good, and a context for understanding and appreciating true beauty. Ultimately, he believed that this came not through the analyzing of nature, but from the examination of the human mind and the soul of man and their tethering to the God who had designed

29. Balfour, *Theism and Humanism*.
30. Lewis, *Is Theology Poetry?*, 4.

them. In this context, after examining the evidence and probabilities that favored design over randomness, Balfour contends that theism makes more sense than any humanistic alternative.

His series of lectures establishing his theistic case covered topics such as "Natural Beauty"; "Values and Higher Emotions"; "Ethics and Theism"; "Reason and Causation"; "Reason and Empirical Agnosticism"; "Mathematicians and Probability"; "Humanism and Theism"; and "Is This Systematic Philosophy?" The following statement sums up Balfour's thesis and the gist of the lectures beautifully:

> And as it is only in a theistic setting that beauty can retain its deepest meaning, and love its brightest lustre, so these great truths of aesthetics and ethics are but half truths, isolated and imperfect, unless we add them to yet a third. We must hold that reason and the works of reason have their source in God; that from Him they draw their inspiration; and that if they repudiate their origin, by this very act they proclaim their own insufficiency.[31]

Lewis repeatedly and consistently visits and re-visits this theme in his own writings, especially in *Mere Christianity* as he points to the fact that it is from inside the context of belief that things begin to become most clear:

> You may ask what good will it be to us if we do not understand it. But that is easily answered. A man can eat his dinner without understanding exactly how food nourishes him. A man can accept what Christ has done without knowing how it works: indeed, he certainly would not know how it works until he has accepted it.[32]

For Balfour in *Theism and Humanism* and for Lewis in *Mere Christianity*, belief gives the ultimate context. And ultimately, that context is a personal and theistic one, expressed most powerfully in the person of Jesus Christ. In that context, the mind, the soul, and that which is orderly and beautiful in this life make the most sense.

31. Balfour, *Theism and Humanism*, 274.
32. Lewis, *Mere Christianity*, 55.

Why Lewis?

Undoubtedly, by reading the summations of the books on The List and Lewis's own thoughts about them, one can see how and why he thought and expressed himself in the manner in which he did—a manner that has impacted countless minds and lives. I challenge you once again to engage with these works for yourself. Imagine with MacDonald, Virgil, and Williams; remember with Boswell; reason with Chesterton, Otto, Balfour, and Boethius; and rhyme with Wordsworth and Herbert, consistently pointing towards the One who is reason and rhyme personified. Once you have done so, you will be poised, prepared, and piqued for reason #6 in my cumulative case.

Reason #6

Because He Believed in the True Myth

For light years and geological periods are mere
arithmetic until the shadow of man, the poet,
the maker of myths, falls upon them.[1]

C. S. LEWIS

Myths and Makers of Myths

THE "MAKER OF MYTHS"? Who is he? He is the One who makes
sense of the grandest and truest telling of the story of humanity,
by giving it language. He gives context to the geological periods,
mathematics, and science that make up the facts of how the story
works. This is what Lewis did so brilliantly. He did not ignore science, order, and rhythm, but through the vehicle of mythical fiction, he endeavored to give context and vibrancy to the brute facts.
As I have stated earlier, he held that in order to give context and
life to the facts, one needs imagination, and imagination was in
fact given to man by the most creative and imaginative One, God
Himself . . . the Original Poet and Storyteller. For He is the Great
Storyteller and Myth Maker, and He has used men from time immemorial and in every culture to tell *the* true story.

1. Lewis, *Miracles*, 52–53.

While Lewis was certainly a great myth-maker and storyteller who used his literary gifts to write myths and stories
that have impacted young and old alike on behalf of Christianity, credit must be given to arguably one of the most ingenious
writers of myths, at least in the modern period (perhaps in all
of human literary history), J. R. R. Tolkien. For it was Tolkien
himself who piqued Lewis's belief in Christianity by challenging him to consider it as the "true myth."[2] However, I must say
that if it were not for my engaging with Lewis, I would not have
known about Tolkien's deep understanding and apologetic use of
myth, especially in relation to Lewis coming to believe in it as the
true myth. That's why, reason #6, *because he believed in the true
myth*, is part of my cumulative case. Since Lewis believed in and
presented the true myth so palpably, we have not only met him,
but we have met his legendary friends as well, and together we
have all become participants in that eternal and true Christian
myth with them.

Mythopoeia

Lewis's belief in the true myth actually came about when he (an
avowed atheist at the time) and Tolkien were engaging in deep
conversations about the power of myths. Lewis, in the heat of
their intellectual battle on September 19, 1931, commented that
myths were merely "lies breathed through silver,"[3] meaning that
there was nothing true about them, albeit they were sometimes
conveyed in beautiful and eloquent fashion. He would point to
The Aeneid,[4] *The Epic of Gilgamesh*, Balder, Osiris, and other such

2. While the term *myth* has been difficult for some to accept, in a literary
and historical context it actually means a traditional story, especially one concerning the early history of a people. Most myths are far-fetched, imaginative,
fanciful, and totally fictitious. Tolkien's point to Lewis was that Christianity
had some of the same elements, but was truthful, hence, it is the "true myth."

3. Carpenter, *Inklings*, 42–45.

4. *The Aeneid* is one of many ancient examples pointing toward the understanding of the true myth that will be discussed. Throughout Christian history,
from the Church Fathers to the present day, Virgil was/is seen as having been

mythologies and mythological figures as examples. In reaction to this statement, Tolkien went home and penned 148 lines of classic poetry that he entitled "Mythopoeia" or myth-maker. Beginning with these now famous words, "Philomythus [myth-lover] to Misomythus [myth-hater] aka Mythopoeia, by J. R. R. Tolkien, To one who said that myths were lies and therefore worthless, even though 'breathed through silver.'"[5] The poem was instrumental in drawing Lewis toward belief in Christianity as truth. The discovery was so powerful an epiphany that only a month later Lewis would write on October 18, 1931, to his good friend Arthur Greeves:

> Now the story of Christ is simply a true myth: a myth working on us in the same way as the others, but with this tremendous difference that it really happened: and one must be content to accept it in the same way, remembering that it is God's myth where the others are men's myths: i.e. the Pagan stories are God expressing Himself through the minds of poets, using such images as He found there, while Christianity is God expressing Himself through what we call "real things." Therefore it is true ... [6]

Over the years Lewis would refine and restate his understanding of the true myth innumerable times and in varied forms. He does so beautifully and succinctly in an essay entitled "Myth Became Fact":

> The heart of Christianity is a myth which is also a fact. The old myth of the Dying God, without ceasing to be myth, comes down from the heaven of legend and imagination to the earth of history. It happens—at a particular date, in a particular place, followed by definable historical consequences. We pass from a Balder or an Osiris dying nobody knows when or where, to a historical person crucified (it is all in order) under Pontius Pilate. By becoming

---

prophetic in some of his language, especially in his *Eclogues*. For a more detailed treatment of this issue, see Ella Bourne, "Messianic Prophecy."

5. Tolkien *Tree and Leaf*, 83.

6. Lewis, *Letters of C. S. Lewis to Arthur Greeves*, 427; letter dated October 18, 1931.

fact it does not cease to be myth: that is the miracle. I suspect that men have sometimes derived more spiritual sustenance from myths they did not believe than from the religion they professed. To be truly Christian we must both assent to the historical fact and also receive the myth (fact though it has become) with the same imaginative embrace which we accord to all myths. The one is hardly more necessary than the other.[7]

In his essay "On Fairy Stories," Tolkien would in fact invent a term that expresses what lies at the center of the understanding of the true myth:

> I will call it Eucatastrophe. The eucatastrophic tale is the true form of fairytale, and its highest function.. . . The Birth of Christ is the eucatastrophe of Man's history. The Resurrection is the eucatastrophe of the story of the Incarnation. This story begins and ends in joy. It has preeminently the "Inner consistency of reality." There is no tale ever told that men would rather find was true, and none which so many sceptical men have accepted as true on its own merit. For the Art of it has the supremely convincing tone of Primary Art, that is, of Creation. To reject it leads either to sadness or to wrath.[8]

The mythopoeic, eucatastrophic, truthful telling of the most important story ever, Christianity, is what spurred these brilliantly gifted men to live, write, and create their joy-spawning, hope-inducing, redemptive works into culture.[9] Thus, through Lewis's

---

7. Lewis, "Myth Became Fact," 63–67. This essay first appeared in *World Dominion*, XXII (September–October 1944), 267–70.

8. Tolkien, "On Fairy Stories."

9. For an additional discussion on issues pertaining to the true myth, the reader is encouraged to refer to Lewis's Appendix in *The Abolition of Man*, 83–101, where he presents what he calls "The Tao." The Tao, or The Way, what Lewis believes is the Natural or Moral Law has flowed into most cultures from one initial, true culture. For a more in-depth study of the idea of "One" initial, monotheistic culture that has most truthfully told the True Myth, the reader is encouraged to refer to Rudolf Otto's *The Idea of the Holy*. Another author who has effectively presented the True Myth in a missiological and evangelistic context is Don Richardson in his book entitled *Eternity in Their Hearts*.

eyes, all men are to be seen as engaged in and living out the grandest and most extraordinary of *all* myths, and the stage is set for reason #7 in my cumulative case.

Reason #7

Because He Was Not Ordinary

There are no ordinary people. You have never talked to a
mere mortal. Nations, cultures, arts, civilizations—these
are mortal, and their life is to ours as the life of a gnat.
But it is immortals whom we joke with, work with, marry,
snub and exploit—immortal horrors or everlasting
splendors. . . . Next to the Blessed Sacrament itself, your
neighbor is the holiest object presented to your senses.[1]

C. S. LEWIS

I KNOW THAT I am stating the obvious here, but I have argued in
my cumulative case from reasons #1 to #6, that Lewis was certainly
anything but ordinary. However, I still think that he would have
said that he was. In fact, Walter Hooper remarked that he (Lewis)
felt that he would recede into relative obscurity within several years
of his death.[2] He was certainly wrong on that one, wasn't he? You
might say, "Well, that's because he was Lewis, the brilliant writer,
scholar, and friend of legends like Tolkien and Williams." I'm still

1. Lewis, *Weight of Glory*, 46.
2. Hooper, "Life and Writing of C. S. Lewis: Part One." In his interview
with Eric Metaxas, Hooper recounts a conversation with C. S. Lewis where he
heard Lewis state that his works and influence would tail off after three years.

going to have to say that I think he saw himself as ordinarily un-ordinary—just a regular guy, who possessed the regular/irregular, unextraordinary/extraordinary, inglorious/glory-filled presence of the Immortal Creator who can use any and all of His imperfect, being-perfected creations in whichever manner He pleases. Lewis would also contend that every one of our neighbors has this paradoxical and weighty nature as well. He emphasizes this beautifully in the quote above, taken from an essay entitled "The Weight of Glory,"[3] which was actually the script of a sermon by the same name, considered by many as one of the best delivered sermons in the modern era and quite possibly ever. And, that is why reason #7, *because he was not ordinary*, has been included in my cumulative case and will stand as its capstone.

The History

On June 8, 1941, in Oxford, at The University Church of St Mary the Virgin, C. S. Lewis delivered the Solemn Evensong sermon, entitled "The Weight of Glory." The church building itself is rife with history. In the sixteenth century, Archbishop Cranmer and bishops Latimer and Ridley were all tried for heresy inside and eventually executed outside on Broad Street not far away. In the eighteenth century, John Wesley attended sermons in the church as an undergraduate student and later preached from its storied pulpit. Walter Hooper recounts that on that Sunday in June 1941 when Lewis delivered his sermon, the crowd at Evensong was one of the largest to assemble there in modern history.[4] The sermon itself, in printed form, is just over 5,300 words and took Lewis about forty-five minutes to deliver, yet its reverberating effects have been resounding ever since.[5]

3. Lewis, *Weight of Glory*, 25–46.

4. Hooper, "Introduction."

5. If you have not already done so, it would behoove you to read the sermon before proceeding any further in this chapter as the remarks that follow will have a fuller context.

The Thesis

The primary text Lewis engaged in his sermon was 2 Cor 4:17, "For our light affliction, which is but for a moment, worketh for us a far more exceeding and eternal weight of glory" (KJV). While Lewis, or a lay reader, would have read the text before the sermon was delivered, he never overtly, verbally refers to it in the body of his sermon again. His palpable, methodical, and convicting remarks repeatedly pointed to the primary truth of his text so powerfully that he didn't need to. A myriad of brilliant illustrations elucidate God's glory expressed in humanity. His thesis is plain: If you are a human being, created in His image, then the potential resides in you to be a god or goddess. The sermon begs the question: "How might one respond under such weight?"

Responses to Glory

Lewis's first suggested response is that we are far too flippant with the fact that God's eternal presence and purpose is in, on, and around us all:

> We are half hearted creatures, fooling about with drink and sex and ambition when infinite joy is offered us, like an ignorant child who wants to go on making mud pies in a slum because he cannot imagine what is meant by the offer of a holiday at the sea. We are far too easily pleased.[6]

The weighty, glory-filled presence is far too powerful, unordinary, and heavy to merely slide through life and focus upon temporal things. While the temporal is present and real, it is not the most important, nor is it the most real. It is only a hint of what is to come, and we cannot get caught up in the pursuit or worship of it.

Second, Lewis suggests that we must understand the promises of Scripture: (1) that we will be with Christ; (2) that we will be like Him; (3) that we will have "glory"; (4) that we will be fed, feasted, and entertained; and (5) that we will have some sort of

6. Lewis, *Weight of Glory*, 26.

ruling position.[7] These promises, throughout the canon of Scripture, repeatedly affirm the weighty presence, power, and purpose of God in us. A presence that is most assuredly not ordinary, nor would it warrant an ordinary, flippant response.

Third, Lewis focuses upon the promise of glory; for this, in his mind, is where things truly and ultimately fall into place. The place where God is pleased with you and welcomes you into "the heart of things."[8] He wonders whether such an audacious scriptural promise that "we shall have *glory*"[9] is an impediment for some and seems contrary to that for which most people feel they should be longing as humble followers of Jesus. However, the statement, "If God is satisfied with the work, that work may be satisfied with itself,"[10] compels us to long for and accept His glory, as well as to offer it to our neighbor. This means loving others as I love myself (Mark 12:31), not in meager, emaciated, and paltry fashion, but with the ostentatious and glorious nature of the lavish love of the Creator Himself (1 John 3:1). This is a glorious and weighty charge. But how can we do this?

We can't. It is literally impossible and too heavy to carry in and of ourselves. This type of glory can only be carried by Jesus and the weight of the cross that He bore on His back. If we try and pridefully carry it ourselves, we fight against the power of the cross and live crushed lives. However, in yielding to His power and strength, we can honor our Lord and our neighbor by bearing the weight of his glory on our own backs. When we do this, we are acting like the gods and goddesses that we were created to be. Lewis reminds us:

> The cross comes before the crown and tomorrow is a Monday morning. A cleft has been opened in the pitiless walls of the world, and we are invited to follow our great Captain inside.[11]

7. Lewis, *Weight of Glory*, 34.

8. Lewis, *Weight of Glory*, 41.

9. Lewis, *Weight of Glory*, 34.

10. Lewis, *Weight of Glory*, 38.

11. Lewis, *Weight of Glory*, 45.

And when we follow the Captain Jesus inside, and ultimately out of that rocky tomb, we are living in the weight of glory. His, our neighbor's, and our own. Glory to His name. The One that is above all names. He gets the ultimate glory, and those of us who are in Him become so luminous that He is all that can be seen when the Father, or anyone else for that matter, beholds us.

Peter Kreeft poignantly articulates these sentiments in his classic book, *Heaven: The Heart's Deepest Longing*:

> There is no escape from the glory, for the glory is the glory of God, and there is no escape from God . . . it calls us to waken to Ultimate Reality. We can think of it as airy and insubstantial, like the creatures in The Tempest, while in fact it is the "enormous bliss of Eden", bigger than a twenty-billion-light-year universe of a trillion trillion suns and heavier than death. And stronger too.[12]

Lewis was not ordinary; neither are we. In fact, no one is, and it is a degrading and demeaning fight to endeavor to be so. That is why there are so many who are sad and mad and filled with hate. The sad, mad, hateful life is uncomfortable and doesn't fit. It isn't what we were created for. We were made for, weighted with, and equipped to carry glory. And when we do, His fame is our fame, and it is infinitely beautiful and luminous and hardly ordinary.

12. Kreeft, *Heaven*, 235.

Conclusion

Are You Convinced?

WELL, HAVE I MADE my case? Was C.S. Lewis, in fact, the second most influential author in modern Christian history? If not, then who was? Who has sold as many or more books than he? Who has been quoted more times than he? Who has introduced us to more literary, philosophical, theological, and historical giants than he? Which author has impacted radio, television, and the big screen more than he (without the aid of the internet)? Who has been as able to write in the genres of fiction, nonfiction, and poetry more profoundly than he? Who has given us more rational, imaginative, and compelling explanations of the Christian faith than he?

While you may have been able to think of several authors who have made profound impacts; who continues to stimulate in the manner that Lewis does? Only recently, more than fifty years after his death, author Michael Ward has made a very compelling claim in his book, *Planet Narnia*, that Lewis had embedded a hidden code in the *Chronicles of Narnia*. A code that points toward Lewis utilizing medieval planetary symbolism in each of the *Chronicles*. Ward's discovery is considered groundbreaking and a testament to the fact that Lewis is still impacting the scholarly and literary worlds profoundly.

Finally, due to the fact that he has inspired us to have this conversation, we are proving, or at least substantiating my thesis. There is simply no one, or at least very few quite like Lewis. This was recently affirmed once again as he was honored on the fiftieth anniversary of his death (November 22, 2013) with his name and a quote being inscribed into the prestigious Poet's Corner in Westminster Abbey. His memory rests eternally and rightfully with the likes of Chaucer, Shakespeare, Dickens, and Kipling. The inscription, one of his most famous utterances affirms his heaven-sent ability to paint an eternal and mythological picture that simply, yet profoundly resonates as true, "I believe in Christianity as I believe the sun has risen. Not only because I can see it but because by it I can see everything else."[1]

1. "C.S. Lewis honoured with Poet's Corner Memorial."

Appendix

Suggested Reading List

THE FOLLOWING AUTHORS EITHER write about Lewis, in Lewisian style, or both. Some are writers of fiction, some nonfiction, and some apologetics. I have no doubt that if you engage with them, a passion will be ignited in you to know and make known the One who is good but not safe and is always on the move.

G. K. Chesterton
Orthodoxy
Father Brown: The Essential Tales
The Man Who Knew Too Much

Walter Hooper
C. S. Lewis: A Companion and Guide
C. S. Lewis: A Biography
C. S. Lewis: Views From Wake Forest

Thomas Howard
Chance or the Dance?
Hallowed Be This House
Narnia and Beyond

Appendix

Timothy Keller
The Reason for God
Jesus the King
Walking with God through Pain and Suffering

John C. Lennox
Seven Days That Divide the World
God's Undertaker: Has Science Buried God?
Gunning for God: Why the New Atheists Are Missing the Target

George MacDonald
The Golden Key
Diary of an Old Soul

Eric Metaxas
Miracles
*Everything Else You Always Wanted to Know About God
    (But Were Afraid to Ask)*
Amazing Grace

Dorothy Sayers
Letters to a Diminished Church
The Mind of the Maker

Bibliography

Articles and Papers

Ahlquist, Dale. "G. K. Chesterton & C. S. Lewis: Chesterton and Lewis Side by Side." *St. Austin Review* (May/June 2013) 4–5. https://staustinreview.org/g_k_chesterton_and_c_s_lewis/.

"Books That Have Influenced: A Preface to a New *Christian Century* Feature." *The Christian Century* (May 2, 1962) 575–76.

Bourne, Ella. "The Messianic Prophecy in Vergil's Fourth Eclogue." *The Classical Journal* 11, no. 7 (April 1916) 390–400. https://www.jstor.org/stable/3287925.

Brown, Devin. Review of *C. S. Lewis and the Church: Essays in Honour of Walter Hooper,* by Judith Wolfe and Brendan Wolfe. *Religion & Literature* 44, no. 1 (Spring 2012) 209–11.

Hanbury, Aaron Cline. "Why C. S. Lewis Never Goes Out of Style." *The Atlantic* (December 17, 2013). https://www.theatlantic.com/entertainment/archive/2013/12/why-cs-lewis-never-goes-out-of-style/282351/.

Lewis, C. S. "Ex Libris." *The Christian Century* 79 (June 6, 1962) 719.

Theroux, David J. "Why C. S. Lewis Is as Influential as Ever." The Independent Institute (August 3, 2015). http://www.independent.org/issues/article.asp?id=7468.

Websites

Bassham, Gregory. "The Anscombe 'Legend' Is Mostly True." Academia, November 22, 2019. https://www.academia.edu/22615497/The_Anscombe_Legend_Is_Mostly_True.

"Books of the Century." *Christianity Today*, April 24, 2000. https://www.christianitytoday.com/ct/2000/april24/5.92.html.

"C. S. Lewis: A Gallery of Family and Friends." *Christianity Today* 7 (1985). https://www.christianitytoday.com/history/issues/issue-7/cs-lewis-gallery-of-family-and-friends.html.

Bibliography

Glyer, Diana. "C. S. Lewis, J. R. R. Tolkien, and the Inklings." C. S. Lewis (website), April 16, 2009. http://www.cslewis.com/c-s-lewis-j-r-r-tolkien-and-the-inklings/.

Higgins, James E. "A Letter from C. S. Lewis." The Horn Book, October 19, 1966. https://www.hbook.com/?detailStory=a-letter-from-c-s-lewis.

Hooper, Walter. "The Life and Writing of C. S. Lewis: Part One." Interview by Eric Metaxas. Socrates in the City. Accessed April 29, 2020. https://socratesinthecity.com/watch/the-life-and-writing-of-c-s-lewis-part-one/.

———. "The Life and Writing of C. S. Lewis: Part Three." Interview by Eric Metaxas. Socrates in the City. Accessed April 29, 2020. https://socratesinthecity.com/watch/the-life-and-writing-of-c-s-lewis-part-three/.

Lambert, Angela. "C. S. Lewis' Other American." Independent, March 7, 1994. https://www.independent.co.uk/life-style/c-s-lewiss-other-american-in-1954-walter-hooper-picked-something-up-he-hasnt-put-it-down-yet-angela-1427576.html.

Lewis, C. S. "Fern-Seed and Elephants." Orthodox Web, 1998. http://orthodox-web.tripod.com/papers/fern_seed.html.

Root, Jerry. "Dispelling Myths about C. S. Lewis." C. S. Lewis (website), January 11, 2016. http://www.cslewis.com/dispelling-myths-about-c-s-lewis/.

Sharp, Rob. "Rescued from the Bonfire, the Lost Work of C. S. Lewis." Independent, March 4, 2011. https://www.independent.co.uk/arts-entertainment/books/news/rescued-from-the-bonfire-the-lost-work-of-c-s-lewis-2231809.html.

Stout, Andrew C. "'It was Allowed to One': C. S. Lewis on the Practice of Substitution." Academia, accessed April 29, 2020. https://www.academia.edu/29444301/_It_Was_Allowed_to_One_C._S._Lewis_on_the_Practice_of_Substitution.

Tolkien, J. R. R. "On Fairy Stories." Brainstorm Services, accessed April 29, 2020. http://brainstorm-services.com/wcu-2005/pdf/fairystories-tolkien.pdf.

Books

Anscombe, G. E. M. Metaphysics and the Philosophy of Mind. Vol. 2 of The Collected Papers of G. E. M. Anscombe. Minneapolis: University of Minnesota Press, 1981.

Balfour, Arthur. Theism and Humanism. Coppel, TX: Forgotten Books, 2012.

Boethius. The Consolation of Philosophy. Translated by P. G. Walsh. Oxford: Oxford University Press, 1999.

Boswell, James. The Life of Samuel Johnson. Oxford: Oxford University Press, 1998.

Carpenter, Humphrey. The Inklings: C. S. Lewis, J. R. R. Tolkien, Charles William and Their Friends. London: HarperCollins, 2006.

Chesterton, G. K. The Everlasting Man. New York: Dodd, Mead & Co., 1925.

Bibliography

Dorsett, Lyle W. *And God Came In: The Extraordinary Story of Joy Davidman.* New York: Macmillan, 1983.

Duriez, Colin. *Tolkien and C. S. Lewis: The Gift of Friendship.* Mahwah, NJ: Hidden Spring, 2003.

Glenday, Craig, ed. *Guinness Book of World Records: 2015.* New York: Random House, 2015.

Green, Roger Lancelyn, and Walter Hooper. *C. S. Lewis: A Bigraphy.* San Diego: Harcourt, 1974.

Gresham, Douglas H. *Lenten Lands: My Childhood with Joy Davidman and C. S. Lewis.* New York: HarperCollins, 1988.

Herbert, George. *The Temple.* London: Penguin Classics, 2017.

Hinten, Marvin D. *The Keys to the Chronicles: Unlocking the Symbols of C. S. Lewis's Narnia.* Nashville: Broadman & Holman, 2005.

Hooper, Walter. "Introduction." In *The Weight of Glory,* by C. S. Lewis. New York: HarperOne/HarperCollins, 2001.

Kreeft, Peter. *Heaven: The Heart's Deepest Longing.* San Francisco: Ignatius, 1989.

———. "Lewis and the Two Roads to God." In *The World and I: A Chronicle of Our Changing Era,* 354–62. Washington, DC: Washington Times, 1987.

Lewis, C. S. *The Abolition of Man.* New York: HarperOne/HarperCollins, 2000.

———. "Bluspels and Flalansferes." In *Rehabilitations and Other Essays,* by C. S. Lewis, 133–58. Oxford: Oxford University Press, 1939.

———. *The Collected Letters of C. S. Lewis: Books, Broadcasts, and the War 1931–1949.* Vol. 2. Edited by Walter Hooper. San Francisco: HarperCollins, 2004.

———. *The Collected Letters of C. S. Lewis: Narnia, Cambridge, and Joy 1950–1963.* Vol. 3. Edited by Walter Hooper. San Francisco: HarperCollins, 2007.

———. *The Discarded Image: An Introduction to Medieval and Renaissance Literature.* Cambridge: Cambridge University Press, 1994.

———., ed. *Essays Presented to Charles Williams.* Oxford: Oxford University Press, 1947.

———. "Introduction." In *On The Incarnation: St. Athanasius,* by St. Athanasius. New York: St. Vladimir's Seminary Press, 2011.

———. *Is Theology Poetry?* Quebec: Samizdat University Press, 2014.

———. *The Last Battle.* New York: Collier, 1970.

———. *The Letters of C. S. Lewis to Arthur Greeves: They Stand Together (1914–1963).* Edited by Walter Hooper. New York: Collier/Macmillan, 1986.

———. *Letters to Malcolm: Chiefly on Prayer.* New York: Harcourt, 1964.

———. *The Lion, the Witch and the Wardrobe.* New York: HarperCollins, 1978.

———. *Mere Christianity.* San Francisco: HarperCollins, 2001.

———. *Miracles.* New York: Macmillan, 1960.

———. "Myth Became Fact." In *God in the Dock: Essays on Theology and Ethics.* Edited by Walter Hooper. Grand Rapids, MI: William B. Eerdmans, 1970.

Bibliography

———. "Preface." In *George MacDonald: An Anthology,* by George MacDonald. New York: HarperOne, 1973.

———. *A Preface to Paradise Lost.* London: Oxford University Press, 1942.

———. *The Problem of Pain.* New York: HarperOne, 2009.

———. *Surprised by Joy: The Shape of My Early Life.* New York: Harcourt Brace Jovanovich, 1955.

———. *The Weight of Glory.* New York: HarperOne/HarperCollins, 2001.

Locke, John. *An Essay Concerning Human Understanding.* New York: Dover, 1959.

MacDonald, George. *George MacDonald: An Anthology.* New York: HarperOne, 1973.

MacDonald, George. *Phantastes.* UK: Smith Elder & Co., 1858.

McGrath, Alister. *C. S. Lewis: A Life.* Colorado Springs: Tyndale, 2013.

Otto, Rudolph. *The Idea of the Holy.* London: Oxford University Press, 1958.

Richardson, Don. *Eternity in Their Hearts.* South Bloomington, MN: Baker, 1981.

Ritter, Mary. "William Wordsworth, *The Prelude.*" In *C. S. Lewis's List: The Ten Books That Influenced Him Most,* edited by David Werther and Susan Werther, 93–112. New York: Bloomsbury Academic, 2015.

Sayer, George. *Jack: A Life of C. S. Lewis.* Wheaton, IL: Crossway, 1994.

Tolkien, J. R. R. *Tree and Leaf: Including Mythopoeia and The Homecoming of Beorhtnoth.* Hammersmith: HarperCollins, 2001.

Vanauken, Sheldon. *A Severe Mercy.* New York: Harper, 1977.

Virgil. *The Aeneid.* Translated by W. F. Jackson Knight. Hammondsworth: Penguin Books, 1958.

Werther, David, and Susan Werther, eds. *C. S. Lewis's List: The Ten Books That Influenced Him Most.* New York: Bloomsbury Academic, 2015.

Williams, Charles. *Descent into Hell.* UK: Faber and Faber, 1937.

Wordsworth, William. *The Prelude.* New York: Norton, 1979.